WEBER'S GUIDE TO
Pipes
AND PIPE SMOKING

WEBER'S GUIDE TO Pipes AND PIPE SMOKING

A Rutledge Book

Bantam Books Edition © 1965 by Bantam Books, Inc.

Prepared by Specialized Publishing Company

Library of Congress Catalog Card Number 65-20629
Printed in the United States of America

This edition published by Rutledge Books,
300 Mercer Street, New York, New York 10003

ISBN: 0-87469-037-4

FOREWORD

So profound are the pleasures of smoking that one must both regret and resent the dictionary definition of the pipe that is content to describe the pipe merely as "a tube of clay, wood, hard rubber or other material, with a small bowl at one end, used for smoking tobacco."

Such a definition is as frustratingly incomplete as calling a sea "a large body of water," or a nightingale "a small old-world migratory bird." If the pipe, which has been man's boon companion for a goodly thousand years or more, deserves a better definition, what is it to be? I leave the decision to phrase-makers, being content to remain a pipemaker, an activity that has happily occupied me for over fifty years. I would, however, subscribe cheerfully to any definition that includes the word "pleasure," for the pipe and the smoking of a pipe, in every aspect, afford pleasure.

The appearance of a pipe—and especially a briar pipe—appeals; grain, bowl, shank and stem have been selected and crafted to seduce the eye. As for the rich taste and full flavor of a finely blended tobacco, and the blossoming bouquet of smoke curling quietly from the bowl, one can only say *voilà!* Contentment is at hand.

In short, pipe smoking is pure pleasure; just ask

the man who smokes one. It is to those who would learn or further extend their knowledge of the pleasures of pipe smoking that this book is dedicated—with the caution that no single book can of itself completely define the pleasures of pipe smoking. As a sea must be voyaged if it is to be fathomed, or a nightingale happened upon if it is to delight, so must a pipe be smoked in order to be fully appreciated.

A word of advice, then: as you read this book, smoke a pipe and savor the pleasure both will provide, for books and pipes are the most suitable of companions, a friendship acknowledged long ago by poet James Thomson.

He wrote:

> *Give a man a pipe he can smoke,*
> *Give a man a book he can read:*
> *And his home is bright with a calm delight,*
> *Though the room be poor indeed.*

CARL WEBER

CONTENTS

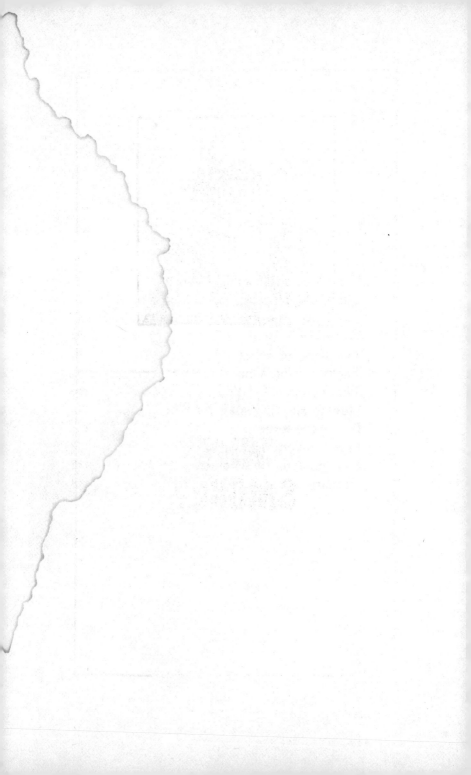

CHAPTER 1

WHY SMOKE?

WHY SMOKE? No one really knows why, though theories are as abundant as the number of brands of cigarettes, cigars, and pipe tobaccos on the market. It may be safely said, however, that the majority of smokers smoke because they enjoy it. A few may complain of their inability to discontinue the habit, but these smokers are, for the most part, veteran cigarette smokers distressed by the hotly debated question, "Does smoking cause cancer?"—a question that will be discussed in depth and detail in the next chapter.

People smoke because they like to. Motivational studies, reports on the personality factors that characterize the smoker, essays on the psychosocial, behavioral, and other aspects of smoking have engendered controversies as confusing as those about sex.

Public Health Service Publication No. 1103, the now-famous Surgeon General's report, *Smoking and Health*, contends that while many investigators have attempted to define the smoker's personality, such a definition ". . . has not emerged from the results so far published in literature." Although this part of the 387-page report deals almost exclusively with cigarette smoking, the conclusions should provide food for thought for the man held to be the most philosophical of smokers—the pipe smoker.

One positive conclusion offered by the Surgeon General's report is that stress seems to be related to smoking, as it is to a score of other habits. The report claims that "there is additional evidence that the experience of stressful situations contributes to the beginning of the habit, to its continuation and to the (amount) consumed."

Following a cautious discussion of the possible relation between stress and tension on the one hand, and smoking behavior on the other, the report poses the troublesome questions: "Is smoking merely an expression of tension, or does it serve as a reducer of psychic tension?" and ". . . would tension actually be less while smoking . . . than while not doing so?"

Of more direct interest to the pipe smoker are some of the studies described by the report. Almost without exception, they tend to paint a flattering picture of the pipester. One study found that pipe smokers have fewer psychosomatic disorders than "heavy, medium and ex-smokers of cigarettes." The Surgeon General's report, it should be pointed out, does not consider the differences "statistically significant."

Another report suggests that "inhaling may be more prevalent among the more neurotic and emotionally disturbed," a comment likely to invite a complacent smile from the noninhaling pipe smoker. In still another study, the general picture of the cigarette smoker is one of a person who tends to "live faster and more intensely" than the man committed to a pipe. On television this may create a romantic image, but in real life it becomes perhaps a more neurotic one, with which the pipe smoker is content not to be identified. It may be argued that modern scientific evidence tends to confirm the impression that the pipe smoker is the less hurried, less worried, and more fully mature man.

In support of this argument is the theory of a world-famous manufacturer of pipes, who argues:

> The pleasure of pipe smoking comes from the taste and aroma of the tobacco and the relaxing overtones of pleasure that create an atmosphere of enjoyment. This has nothing to do with the inhaling of tobacco into the lungs.
> The cigarette smoker's satisfaction comes from a temporary denial of oxygen while the smoke is inhaled into the lungs and a feeling of buoyancy which occurs with the return of oxygen after the inhalation. A pipe (which should not be inhaled) will never provide the same kind of stimulation as cigarette inhaling. The prospective pipe smoker must agree to forego this stimulation and replace it with a milder and more solid form of satisfaction.

Pharmacological research agrees with this theory. The Surgeon General's report quotes one researcher as stating, "The decisive factor in the effects of the tobacco, desired or undesired, is nicotine." The report observes that nicotine, named after Frenchman Jean Nicot, is present in tobacco in significant amounts and affects many organs and structures, including the nervous system, producing in the individual "cellular stimulation followed by depression which is noted in isolated tissue and organ systems."

The report deals extensively with the pharmacological response of the organism to nicotine, describing its various effects on the nervous system, as well as its cardiovascular and gastrointestinal effects. Surprisingly, although the effects of nicotine have a profound influence upon the individual system, nicotine absorption does not, according to the report, represent a significant health problem. One reason advanced for this idea is that the amount of nicotine present in tobacco is very low. Also, nicotine is very rapidly metabolized into nontoxic substances by man and certain other animals. In short, it may be said of nicotine that it makes cigarette smoking pleasurable—indeed, habit-forming—and that while nicotine serves no useful purpose, it does not deserve to be labeled a public enemy. Nicotine appears to affect only the smoker who inhales.

One curious aspect of nicotine is that it may act either as a stimulant or as a tranquilizer, roles that play a much less important part in cigar and pipe smoking than in cigarette smoking. If nicotine acts, at times, as a sedative or tranquilizer, why then do some individuals find the act of smoking stimulating? One theory contends that the so-called stimulation is produced by the bronchial and pulmonary irritations caused by inhaling. Whatever the final results of pharmacological and psychological effects of nicotine on human beings, one fact emerges clearly and indisputably: pipe smokers (and cigar smokers) do not necessarily smoke for the same reasons that motivate—consciously or unconsciously—the cigarette smoker.

Why, then, if it neither stimulates nor tranquilizes as strongly as a cigarette, does one smoke a pipe? The simple, nonpharmacological answer is that it is a pleasurable experience. The prime appeal of the pipe comes from the taste and aroma of the tobacco—sensory gratification. There is also an added sensory experience, the tactile one of holding the pipe in the hand and in the mouth. But a greater pleasure of pipe smoking is a generalized, but measurable, atmosphere of enjoyment.

Beyond the pleasure it affords the senses, a pipe appeals esthetically, philosophically, and therapeutically. Designed for a highly specialized function, a pipe needs only a bowl and stem to fulfill its purpose. These two components may take any imaginable shape and size, as long as the pipe will function. Pipes may be long, short, straight, curved, slender, or fat. They may boast the haughty beauty of the church warden, with its long, clean lines, or arrest the eye with elaborate carvings, as do many briars. Indeed, Napoleon presented a friend with a meerschaum shaped like a mortar being wheeled into action. Ornamented with diamonds, its original value was 30,000 francs. Whether fashioning a pipe from delicate porcelain or from coarsely textured corncob, the pipe maker has, through the centuries, added a dimension of beauty to everyday living.

As for the pipe's appeal to the reflective man, literature is rich with evidence. Each century has prompted a new generation of poet-philosophers to sing the praises of their pipes in paeans that, while sincere, range in quality from pedestrian to Parnassian. The flowering of tobacco-oriented leaves of poetry in the 19th century in particular was truly heroic. Byron, Burns, Scott, Lamb, Tennyson, Thackeray, and Lowell, to name but a few, ranted and rhapsodized. Every smoker knows Lord Bulwer-Lytton's glowing tribute to the pipe in his *Night and Morning*, which appeared in 1841. It is terser and more to the point than most panegyrics: "A pipe! Is a great soother, a pleasant comforter. Blue devils fly before its honest breath. It ripens the brain, it opens the heart; and the man who smokes thinks like and acts like a Samaritan." And anecdotists chime in from the wings of that colorful stage. One story celebrating the philosophical significance attributed to the pipe is recounted by W. G. Hutchinson in his book *Lyra Nicotiana*, published in London in 1898.

Hutchinson wrote, "Think of that eloquently silent evening at Craigenputtock in 1833 when Carlyle and Emerson, on either side of the fireplace, puffed soberly with never a spoken word till midnight and then parted shaking hands with mutual congratulation on the profitable and pleasant evening they had spent."

Apocryphal though this tale may be, the pipe has always been associated with the man of a philosophical turn of mind. Nor has the 20th century altered this image; for example, a famous photograph of Einstein shows him posing in profile with his favorite pipe. That pipe smoking is now enjoying a clearly discernible renaissance may be largely due to its appeal to the "thinking man," to borrow a phrase exploited by a cigarette manufacturer.

It is also possible that smokers are turning to pipes in reaction against the nature of the age in which we live. Although leisure time becomes increasingly abundant, man's use of it, paradoxically, becomes less leisurely. Vacationers jet from place to place; weekend wanderers seek high-speed expressways to quicken their journeys; "instant" foods beckon from the billboards that affront the landscape. In this age of rocketry and gimmickry, the pipe alone has stubbornly resisted technological innovation, requiring, as it always has, hand-stoked fuel and manual ignition.

The pipe, in fact, is at odds with many of the touchstones of Madison Avenue culture. As there is nothing "instant" about it, so there is nothing "disposable." The useful characteristic of disposability has promoted the sale of diapers, dinner napkins, minnow buckets, and even, in a way, automobiles, but it is fundamentally incompatible with the pipe, which is cherished for its durability. A new pipe may outlast all of a man's earthly possessions.

The therapeutic aspects of pipe smoking are

powerful—but difficult to define. They assume, in the aggregate, the proportions of a mystique. Ritual secrecy, superstition, myth, legend, and practices as elaborate and esoteric as voodoo ceremony sometimes attend the use and maintenance of a pipe. In a world obsessed with automation, pipe care may prove to be the last stronghold for the man in search of do-it-yourself therapy. As fishing paraphernalia exercises an almost hypnotic effect upon the angler, so, too, does pipe equipment fascinate the pipe smoker—reamer, sweetener, cleaner, pouch, humidor, rack, tamper, spoon and windcap, curer and cure-all. It may be that one day a formula will be propounded that equates the need to putter with the need to escape the push-button monotony of modern-day life. This is an overstatement, admittedly, but in the care and maintenance of a pipe there is the reward of performing tasks that require manual skill, judgment, deliberation, and experience—acts of tender, loving care that prompted one author to write, "There is something in a pipe that can make a man stable in mind."

Nevertheless—in the face of the accusing arguments marshalled by modern medicine—why smoke?

The pipe smoker can cite the sensory, esthetic, and reflection-inducing virtues of a fine blend in a favorite bowl. And if these fail to convince, no one can dispute his final, defiant proclamation, "I smoke because I enjoy it."

CHAPTER 2

THE
SURGEON
GENERAL'S
REPORT

For thy sake, tobacco, I
Would do anything but die!

THIS GRIM JEST, written by Charles Lamb more than a century ago, might well urge the modern smoker to study the means by which he can remove as much risk as possible from the smoking habit. For to the man or woman willing to do anything in order to enjoy tobacco save die, the Surgeon General's report on *Smoking and Health* indicates a clear course of action: smoke a pipe!

Here in this report are the hard (hard for the cigarette smoker to accept) facts about smoking, obtained from the prolonged study and evaluation of many lines of converging research conducted by the U. S. Department of Health, Education and Welfare.

The most significant and shocking statement in the report appears on page 33, and is the first statement in the book to appear in bold face type: *"Cigarette smoking is a health hazard of sufficient importance in the United States to warrant appropriate remedial action."*

The report stresses that the death rate for smokers of cigarettes only, who were smoking at the time of the particular study covered by the Surgeon General's report, ". . . is about 70 percent higher than that for nonsmokers. The death rates increase with the amount smoked. For groups of men smoking less than 10, 10–19, 20–39, and 40 cigarettes and over per day, respectively, the death rates are about 40 percent, 70 percent, 90 percent, and 120 percent higher than for nonsmokers."

For men smoking five or more cigars daily, death rates were slightly higher (9 percent to 27 percent) than for nonsmokers in the four studies dealing with this information. There is some indication that this higher death rate occurs primarily in men who stated that they inhaled the cigar smoke to some degree.

Death rates for current pipe smokers were little, if at all, higher than those for nonsmokers, and this even applies to men smoking 10 or more pipefuls per day and men who had smoked pipes for more than 30 years.

Now let us compare the relationship of cigarette smoking, then of pipe smoking, to deaths from lung cancer and other diseases, notably coronary artery disease, chronic bronchitis, and emphysema (the major cause of death and disability in the United States, as evidenced by the fact that in 1962 some 500,000 people in the U.S. died of arteriosclerotic heart disease, principally coronary heart disease, 41,000 died of lung cancer, and 15,000 died of bronchitis and emphysema).

The Surgeon General's report states that cigarette smoking is causally related to lung cancer in

men and that the magnitude of the effect of cigarette smoking far outweighs all other factors. The
data for women, though less extensive, point in the
same direction.

The chances of contracting lung cancer increase
with the duration of smoking and the number of
cigarettes smoked per day, and are diminished by
discontinuing smoking. The report states, "The
risk of developing cancer of the lung for the
combined group of pipe smokers, cigar smokers and
pipe and cigar smokers, is greater than for nonsmokers, but much less than for cigarette smokers."

A study of a group of U. S. veterans shows, of
deaths within the group over a given period, the
deaths occurring from various types of lung cancer. (See Table 1.)

Table 2, from the Surgeon General's report, is
a more comprehensive table, based on seven studies
showing mortality ratios for lung cancer by smoking status, type of smoking, and amount smoked.

Additional studies evaluated by the Surgeon General's committee indicate that the cigarette smoker
is more prone to oral cancer than the pipe smoker.
Seven studies revealed that the chances of death
from oral cancer are 4.1 times greater for cigarette
smokers than for nonsmokers. Yet this rate, for
pipe and cigar smokers, 3.3 percent, is a modest
one as compared to such a statistic as that showing
heavy cigarette smokers to have a 34.1 percent
mortality rate for cancer of the lung. Also, the
Surgeon General's report states, hesitantly, that
"the causal relationship of pipe smoking to the de-

TABLE 1

Nonsmokers*	2.0
Pipe and/or cigar smokers	2.8
Cigarette smokers, total†	20.5
Current cigarette smokers,	
less than 20 per day	18.0
more than 20 per day	38.4
Discontinued cigarette smokers (by maximum amount ever smoked),	
less than 20 per day	9.3
more than 20 per day	17.7

* Includes occasional smokers.
† Includes men who smoked pipe and/or cigars in addition to cigarettes.

TABLE 2

Study	Doll and Hill	Hammond and Horn	Dorn	Dunn, Linden and Breslow—Occupational	Dunn, Buell and Breslow—Legion	Best, Josie and Walker	Hammond
Lung cancer deaths in Study	129	448	535	139	98	221	414
Lung cancer deaths Non-smokers	†3	†25	†56	†3	†12	†8	†16
(Reference number)	(83)	(163)	(88)	(96)	(97)	(25)	(157)
MORTALITY RATIOS:							
All Smokers	12.8	10.7	6.0	—	—	*25.2	†8.1
1-14 gm. tobacco	6.7	—	—	—	—	—	—
15-24 gm. tobacco	12.3	—	—	—	—	—	—
25 gm. tobacco	23.7	—	—	—	—	—	—

Current: * *							
Cigarettes only	†9.6	†11.7	†4.9	†15.9	†12.0	†10.0	†20.2
<10	—	†8.4	—	(5)— 8.3	†5.2	†5.8	4.4
10-20	—	†13.5	—	(10)— 9.0	†9.4	†7.3	10.8
21-39	—	} †15.1	—	(20)—19.4	†18.1	†15.9	} 43.7
40+	—		—	(30)—25.1 / (40)—28.7	†23.3	†21.7	
≦1 pack †	—	11.8	4.2	13.6	8.1	6.9	8.1
>1 pack †	—	15.1	7.4	24.1	18.0	16.9	43.8
Pipes only	} †1.5	} †1.1	—	—	1.3 } †1.6	2.6 } †1.3	5.4 } †4.6
Cigars only			—	—	1.5	1.0	
Pipes and cigars	—	†24.4	—	—	6.2	—	9.7
Cigarettes, pipes and cigars	—	—	—	—	—	10.7	—
Occasional	—	—	—	—	—	1.3	—
Ex-Smokers:							
>10 yrs. since stopped							
<20 cigarettes	—	—	—	—	—	2.4	5.0
>20 cigarettes	—	—	—	—	—	17.8	—
<10 yrs. since stopped							
<20 cigarettes	—	—	—	—	—	10.4	8.4
>20 cigarettes	—	—	—	—	—	22.8	—
<20 cigarettes (irrespective of when stopped)	—	—	—	—	†1.3	—	—
>20 cigarettes (irrespective of when stopped)	—	—	—	—	†1.6	—	—

* Current and ex-smokers combined.

† Most recent information.

— Data not available or not available for designated classes.

** Two California studies and current Hammond study include all cigarette smokers (cigarettes and other and current and ex-cigarette smokers).

velopment of cancer of the lip *appears* to be established." (Italics are the author's.)

With regard to cancer of the larynx, the report states that retrospective studies with adequate samples all show cigarette smoking to be the most significant form of smoking associated with the disease, and that the number of cases associated with cigar and pipe smoking was "not yet large enough for judgment."

Research on esophageal cancer discloses that smokers of more than one pack of cigarettes per day have a mortality rate of 4.9 percent; the pipe smoker's is 3.2 percent.

Four studies of cancer of the urinary bladder found significant associations with cigarette smoking. Only two studies found a link with pipe and/or cigar smoking.

Concerning stomach cancer, both cigarette and pipe smokers can exhale with relief—if they have not yet been frightened to death. None of the studies alluded to by the Surgeon General's report shows an association between gastric cancer and smoking of any kind.

The finger of suspicion is again pointed at the cigarette in the portion of the report dealing with nonneoplastic respiratory diseases, particularly chronic bronchitis and pulmonary emphysema. The latter severely disables large numbers of men of working age and, as a direct or contributory cause of death, has a considerable effect upon mortality. Though little is known about the exact composition of cigarette smoke in the respiratory tract after it leaves the mouth, studies have revealed that the inhalation of cigarette smoke produces coughing, sputum, and a reduction in ventilatory function; increases the risk of dying from influenza, pneumonia, and pulmonary emphysema; and "is the most direct cause of chronic bronchitis in the United States."

Because little smoke is inhaled by the pipe smoker, it may be said that pipe smoking plays a smaller role than does cigarette smoking in encouraging those diseases caused, partially or entirely, or aggravated by deposits of smoke constituents in the upper or lower respiratory tracts. In a discussion of the prevalence of respiratory symptoms, the Public Health Service report states, ". . . all [the studies] tend to show that pipe smokers are likely to be intermediate between non-smokers and cigarette smokers in prevalence of symptoms and signs."

In the interest of fair reporting, however, it must be noted that the report says there is reason to believe that pipe smoking, more often than cigarette smoking, may produce certain "non-malignant alterations in the mouth, nose or throat . . . [which] disappear after the cessation of smoking."

For many decades smoking has been denounced as a prime cause of heart disease, but the government report on health and smoking shies away from making definite statements on this subject, save to say that male cigarette smokers have a higher death rate from coronary artery disease than nonsmoking males, but that it is not clear that this association has causal significance. But, once again, pipe smoking seems to be much the safer road for the disciple of the herb to tread. One long-term series of studies of cardiovascular disease in Framingham and in Albany, which featured a painstaking search at regular intervals for clinical manifestations of the disease, showed a threefold increase in the incidence of myocardial infarction and coronary deaths in men who were heavy cigarette smokers as compared to nonsmokers, pipe smokers, and cigar smokers.

If perusal of this chapter does not produce an ulcer in the cigarette smoker, continued cigarette smoking may succeed where this chapter has failed. Studies on the relationship of smoking to gastric and duodenal ulcers show that a direct association with cigarette smoking exists. The Surgeon General's report, however, states, "no association with pipe smoking was noted." In one study, heavy cigarette smokers were found to have a frequency of peptic ulcer twice that of those who had never smoked. Conversely, in a clinical trial it was shown that patients advised to stop smoking cigarettes had an average 78 percent reduction in the size of the ulcer.

The Surgeon General's report is a statistical chamber of horrors, one that cannot help but unnerve the most stoical of cigarette smokers. Yet the purpose of this chapter is not to indict the cigarette, but rather to cheer the pipe owner who may have been smoking more and enjoying it less since the Great Debate began. That the government report repeatedly separates the "cigarette smoker" from "the pipe and/or cigar smoker and non-smoker" is reason enough for the pipe smoker to rejoice.

In fairness to the cigarette industry, however, it must be stated that its spokesmen, following expensive and extensive research conducted privately, take issue with the comments and conclusions of Public Health Service Publication No. 1103, asserting vigorously that there has yet to be established a conclusive and decisive link between cigarette smoking and the health problems discussed in this chapter.

Who is to be believed in the Great Debate—the committee formed by the Surgeon General's office or the numerous researchers obtained by the cigarette industry? Time and further study must decide the issues. Meanwhile, back at the tobacconist's shop, the consumer who wishes to play it safe will surely cast his vote for the pipe. Yet, surprisingly, earlier medical furors over smoking produced few pipe converts.

Since 1900, when per capita consumption in the United States was less than 50 cigarettes per year, cigarette smoking has grown steadily and dramatically. Annual consumption in 1961, for example, was nearly 4,000 cigarettes per person. But during the same period, consumption of pipe tobacco, which had reached a peak of 2½ pounds per person in 1910, slumped to little more than a half a pound per person in 1962. Cigar smoking showed a similar decline.

The 1955 Current Population Survey showed that 68 percent of the male population and 32.4

percent of the female population of 18 years and over were regular cigarette smokers. Why do statistics continue to champion the cigarette and chagrin the cigar and pipe? Some point to the vastly greater amounts of money spent by the cigarette industry on advertising. Others concur with those areas in the Surgeon General's report that suggest that cigarettes and cigarettes alone seem to satisfy the psychological and social drives of most Americans—drives that are reinforced by the pharmacological actions of nicotine on the central nervous system.

In conclusion, the Surgeon General's report, which deals in matters and minutiae too technical to be of interest to the layman, states that the death rate for cigarette smokers only is about 70 percent higher than that for nonsmokers, while death rates for current pipe smokers are little if at all higher than for nonsmokers. On the basis of these statements alone, the case for pipe smoking is a persuasive one—one that should appeal to all who cherish the pipe dream of smoking with a minimum of risk, and one that merits serious consideration on the part of all those smokers who "would do anything but die" for the sake of their tobacco.

CHAPTER 3

THE EARLY HISTORY OF SMOKING

SINCE THE first caveman took pleasure from inhaling the smoke from a fire—quite likely one ignited by lightning—man has been burning something and breathing in its fumes. This "something" has been tobacco for only a comparatively short time: it was introduced to the civilized world less than 500 years ago. Since pipe smoking was known in Europe and the East long before the dawn of written history, it is not surprising that the pipe has been used to burn a bewildering variety of substances, including hemp, narcotics, dried dirt, charcoal, herbs and spices, pepper, and ashes. There is evidence that the Celts smoked spicy herbs in iron pipes, and Indian pipes have been dated as far back as 6,000 years ago.

But the earliest smokers were pipeless. Their preoccupation with smoke was probably rooted in those religious ceremonies in which primitive man worshipped the sun with offerings of holy fire. It is assumed that priests, who spent much of their lives at the altar, wearied of the acrid fumes of foul-smelling substances and initiated the burning of sweet herbs and fragrant gums. This, in turn, led to the discovery of incense, which played an important role in the religious ceremonies of the ancient Mesopotamians and the oldest Egyptian dynasties that lived on the banks of the Nile. When archaeologists unsealed the tomb of Tutankhamen, they found grayish-brown pellets of resin and evidence that such pellets were burned in exquisite alabaster vases as perfumed offerings to the gods. The burning of myrrh and various kinds of incense, according to the inscriptions found in the pyramids, dates back as far as 3,000 B.C.

Both the Old and New Testaments make frequent mention of incense, the best known example being the story of the Magi, or Holy Kings, who brought gold, frankincense, and myrrh to the newborn babe named Jesus. Morning and evening in Old Jerusalem was marked by incense burned before the curtain that hid the Holy of Holies.

In the 6th or 7th century the practice of burning incense to the gods spread to Greece. At Delphi, where priests delivered dark prophecies, a Pythian prophetess was employed to give tongue to the oracles. Showmanship dictated that this mistress of ceremonies inhale fumes from burning barley meal and laurel. The smoke she inhaled dilated her eyes and produced a state of trance, wowing the audience.

The Romans, hasty imitators though they were, waited several centuries before importing incense to burn, though there is evidence that they favored incense as an ingredient in the libations they offered to their gods. Among the Greeks and Romans we get the first indication of smoke being used for medicinal purposes. Hippocrates, the Greek physician who lived at the time of the Peloponnesian War, advocated the inhalation of smoke as the treatment of certain diseases of women. The Romans also insisted that an obstinate cough could be cured with smoke. Enter now Pliny, probably the earliest writer to describe anything resembling a pipe. Regarded as the greatest writer of antiquity on natural history, Pliny wrote 73 books during the reigns of Nero and Vespasian, 12 of which concerned plant-derived medicines. His prescription for a chronic cough was the inhalation of coltsfoot through a reed (*arundo*), a reference that may have been a literary first. It appears that the gods were not very impressed with Pliny's theories, for he was reduced to ashes in the eruption of Vesuvius in A.D. 79, an ignoble end for an early supporter of smoking.

Meanwhile, in the region of the Lower Danube and in countries of the East, narcotic plants were being inhaled with pleasure—perhaps an understatement, for the inhalers generally became stupefied. Herodotus, hoariest and oldest of the Greek historians, once described a "tree which bears the strangest produce." He said that when the Scythian tribesmen of Asia Minor "meet together in companies, they throw some of it upon the fires 'round which they are sitting, and presently, by the mere smell of the fumes which it gives out in burning, they grow drunk as the Greeks do with wine. More of the fruit is then thrown on the fire and, their drunkenness increasing, they jump up and begin to dance and sing." This early account of a hootenanny, circa 450 B.C., may possibly refer to the burning of tobacco, but more likely the Scythians used hemp. Herodotus called the smoke "superior to any Grecian vapour-bath." He further states that the Babylonians too were enamored of this habit.

The burning of hemp seeds after a meal apparently enjoyed, among the ancients, the status of our after-dinner cigar, cigarette, or pipe, for such later writers as Tyrius, Pomponius Mela, and Plutarch speak of this vogue. They report that the inhalation induced a hilarity bordering on intoxication, followed by a torpor and deep slumber. Although there have been many reports of the burning of substances for their narcotic effects, such as the use of opium in the ancient Orient, it must be remembered that there is not a single reference in Greek, Roman, or German legendary history to the practice of smoking as it is known today. In the ancient world the use of smoke was invariably connected with ceremonial or medicinal purposes, or it was a means of producing a stupor.

Smoking as a socially approved means of obtaining personal pleasure was probably born in that part of the world where the tobacco plant originally flourished—in the Antilles and coastal districts of Central America and Mexico, regions boasting ideal climate for the cultivation of tobacco. It appears that the Mayas of Central America, an Indian people who believed in sun-worship and the offering of incense, were the first to recognize the pleasure afforded by burning and smoking tobacco, a plant that grew wild and often attained a luxuriant growth.

The Mayas were a highly developed race. Their temples and buildings were as magnificent as those of ancient Greece. Reliefs in their temples show priests smoking tube-like pipes, and it was apparently not long before smoking became a universal habit. Gradually, the smoking of tobacco and other herbs spread through primitive communities in Central America, Mexico, and the Antilles. In A.D. 620, the Mayan civilization crumbled like pipe ash. The Mayas wandered northward, and their practice of smoking spread rapidly to other tribes.

In the Aztec civilization, before the arrival of the Spaniards, despotic Montezuma held sway. During his reign, according to one historian, a young man was elected each year as the incarnation of one of the deities. For 12 months the youth was allowed to indulge his every desire, and he had "the fairest maidens in the land for his companions." But at the end of the year, "amid dances, flute-playing and the eloquence of orators, his last act, before dying, was to smoke a pipe of tobacco to the glory of the gods and the happiness of mankind." One wonders if this custom gave rise to the expression "paying the piper."

As the Aztecs extended their conquests, pipe smoking spread throughout Central America. Through the raids of the bloodthirsty Caribs, and similar conflicts and colonizations, smoking became popular in Venezuela, Guiana, and Brazil. Although the "weed" had established itself throughout the whole of North and Central America, it was to remain unknown to the greater part of South America until the arrival of the Spanish explorers, coming from a civilization that knew as little about tobacco as it did about the New World. To Christopher Columbus, the redoubtable Genoa-born adventurer, belongs credit for providing us with the first accounts of smoking in America, an honor that might be disputed by the ghosts of certain of the Viking explorers, were they able to produce such accounts of their own.

In his journal Columbus wrote, "Monday, October 25th. . . . Being at sea, about midway between Santa Maria and the large island which I named Fernandina, we met a man in a canoe going from Santa Maria to Fernandina; he had with him . . . some dried leaves which are of high value among them, for a quantity of it was brought to me at San Salvador."

It appears that Columbus and company did not, on that historic day, know to what use the natives put the leaves. But in November, on an island called Cuba, Columbus sent two of his men, Rodrigo de Jerez and Luis de Torres, into the dense tropical vegetation in search of gold. When they returned two weeks later, their reports included mention of natives carrying in their hands dried leaves which they kindled with coals and held to their mouths to inhale and exhale the smoke. These reports would have been lost to us had not Columbus survived a storm that raged off the native shores before his triumphant return to Spain on March 15, 1493. That same year Columbus returned to the

New World accompanied by Romano Pane, a monk ordered by Pope Alexander VI to convert the Indians to Christianity and commissioned by Columbus to write a book about the customs of the New World.

Brother Pane called the practice of smoking "making Cohobba," and describes, in a rather vague fashion, the use of tobacco by priests and medicine men. A more detailed account is that of Gonzalo Fernandez de Oviedo y Valdes, a historian who served with Columbus and then spent 34 years studying the customs and manners of the natives. In his *Historia General y Natural de las Indias*, Oviedo writes,

> Among other evil practices, the Indians have one that is especially harmful, the inhaling of a certain kind of smoke which they call tobacco in order to produce a kind of stupor. . . . The *caciques* (priests) employed a tube shaped like a Y, inserting the forked extremities in their nostrils and the tube itself in the lighted weed; in this way they would inhale the smoke until they became unconscious and lay sprawling on the earth like men in a drunken slumber. Those who could not procure the right sort of wood took their smoke through a hollow reed (*canuela*); it is this that the Indians call *tabacco*, and not the weed nor its effects, as some have supposed. They prize this herb very highly, and plant it in their orchards or on their farms for the purpose mentioned above.

Oviedo goes on to say that he "cannot imagine what pleasure they derive from this practice," one that he labels "a bad and pernicious custom."

Others were quick to echo Oviedo's charge that tobacco smoking was a filthy habit. Jacques Cartier, paddling up the St. Lawrence River in 1535, commented on the natives he observed smoking: "They suck themselves so full of smoke that it oozes from their mouths like smoke from a chimney. They say the habit is most wholesome, but we found that tobacco bit our tongues like pepper."

In 1546 an observer named Benzoni wrote of the Indians, "Smoke goes into mouth, throat and head. They retain it as long as they can, for they find pleasure in it. Some take so much they fall down as though dead and remain stupefied. Others imbibe enough to become giddy and no more."

But as the Indians found pleasure in it, so did the white men who were learning the uses of the weed. It proved itself as capable of making friends as enemies. Indeed, the war between pro- and anti-tobacconists was to be fought on moral grounds well into the 20th century, when the medical aspects of smoking were to assume pre-eminence.

The writings of Pane and Oviedo, the frequent voyages of Spanish explorers to the New World, and, later, the explorations of the Portuguese swiftly made the European nations tobacco-conscious. In the centuries that followed each generation was to produce its men of letters to uphold the pipe as "a sovereign remedy . . . for the degeneracy of the times" or inveigh against it as a "fearful disease."

CHAPTER 4

THE LATER HISTORY OF SMOKING

IN THE YEAR 1559, when smoking was common-place among the Spanish and Portuguese sailors in the various ports, Jean Nicot of France, a private secretary to 15-year-old King Sebastian, arrived in Lisbon with instructions to negotiate a marriage between the King and the daughter of Henry II, 16-year-old Marguerite de Valois.

By this time, tobacco seeds, as well as the dried leaf, had reached Lisbon. The seeds were planted "in pleasure gardens" or grown for medicinal purposes. When a Portuguese friend showed Nicot a tobacco plant grown in a garden, Nicot asked for cuttings. These found their way to the garden of the French Embassy, where they were most welcome, for Nicot had sent word ahead that the plant was supposed to be an effective remedy for a cancerous tumor then called *Noli-me-tangere* and for a variety of "eating sores."

History states that upon his return to France, Nicot, having failed in his role as the King's matchmaker, made good use of the tobacco. He effected several cures with the herb—a chef's cut thumb, a rash on the face of a lady acquaintance, a gentleman's foot, and a variety of ulcers.

Emboldened by his success, Nicot told Cardinal Francis of the remarkable properties of tobacco—

how it had produced miraculous cures in cases of cancer thought to be incurable. Word of the wonder-working weed reached the highly superstitious Queen Mother, Catherine de Medici, whose retinue included magicians, astrologers, and alchemists. She became tobacco's champion, and, in a short while, tobacco came to be known as "the Queen's herb" and the "Medici's plant." A legend also grew and persisted that the Queen was the original inventor of snuff.

Tobacco's fame spread quickly throughout Europe. Nicolo Monardes, physician at the University of Seville, published an account of tobacco, praising it as a cure for coughs, asthma, headaches, gout, stomach cramps, intestinal worms, certain women's diseases, open wounds, and malignant tumors. Nicot, meanwhile, quit politics. Devoting himself to scholarship, he compiled a French dictionary; surprisingly, the work did not contain a single word meaning "to smoke." Yet, in 1570 the brothers Liebault gave the tobacco plant its accepted botanical name *Nicotiana*, after "its original discoverer." In the same year the first botanical book on tobacco was written by Drs. Pena and Lobel and dedicated to their Queen, Elizabeth.

Hailed as a panacea for every ill known to man, tobacco plants passed from the hands of one botanist to another and, by the 1580's, were to be found in botanical gardens in Holland, Switzerland, Italy, Austria, Hungary, Turkey, and Russia. In many places tobacco was cultivated for its medicinal properties, but, whatever the reasons, the world had become tobacconized.

The practice of smoking for pleasure and pleasure alone, with little regard for its alleged medicinal values, originated in England, largely as the result of encounters between the sailors serving under Admirals Hawkins, Drake, and Raleigh and the natives of Central and South America. At first the English explorers, like those before them, misunderstood the object of their curiosity. Hawkins, in the account of his second voyage (1564–1565), said that the natives smoked to appease their hunger and were thus able to go as long as five days without eating or drinking. By 1570, however, chroniclers had already described tobacco as "an inmate of England," and in 1573 a history stated, "In these days the taking-in of smoke of the Indian herb called 'tobaco' (sic) by an instrument formed like a little ladle, whereby it passes from the mouth into the head and stomach, is greatly taken-up and used in England."

Perhaps the most avid pipe smoker of the day was Sir Walter Raleigh, who smoked persistently at court and made many converts there. Queen Elizabeth herself, influenced by Raleigh, tried a pipeful of tobacco. Although her first attempt appears to have been her last, her enemies claimed that she was a heavy smoker, thus reinforcing the rumor that the Queen, an irascible eccentric, was really a man. As the "barbarous habit" became the fashion of London, all manner of pipes flourished, ranging from exquisite pipes wrought from silver to pipes as simple as a walnut shell with a straw for a stem.

Ironically, although the potato was introduced into the Old World at the same time as tobacco, a full century was to pass before its cultivation became popular. Alexander von Humboldt wrote on this paradox: "As an ignorant child, if offered the choice between a piece of bread and a glowing coal, stretches out his hand first to the latter, even so did the people of Europe choose between potatoes and tobacco." Goethe shared Humboldt's view that "two important plants come to us from America, one as a blessing, the other as a curse. The blessing is the potato, the curse is tobacco."

By the end of Elizabeth's reign, smoking had achieved such popularity that there were schools for smokers. Professors of smoking insisted that their pupils be able to inhale smoke through the nose and master the art of blowing smoke rings in the air. With such popularity, the demand for tobacco was soon greater than the supply. As a result, a pound of tobacco cost its weight of silver coins.

Then, one day, Elizabeth, who had no objection to smoking, exhaled her last breath and James I became King of England. At the very outset of his reign, he published a bitter tract against smoking, vowing that he would bring an end to the "disgusting business." Smoking, he declared in his famous *Counter-blaste to Tobacco*, was "stinking and unsavourie. . . ." Furthermore, the King asked his astonished subjects, ". . . shall we, I say, without blushing, abase ourselves so farre as to imitate those beastly Indians? . . . Why doe we not as well imitate them in walking naked as they doe? . . . Yea, why do we not denie God and adore the Devil as they doe?"

But was not tobacco supposed to have healing properties? King James responded with this sarcastic statement: ". . . when a sicke man hath had his disease at the height, hee hath at that instant taken tobacco and afterward, his disease taking the natural course of declining and the patient consequently recovering his health, O then the tobacco, forsooth, was the worker of that miracle." Smokers who enjoyed an after-dinner pipe heard their King rant, ". . . smoke becomes a kitchen far better than a dining chamber." The very aroma of tobacco enraged the King, who compared it with the smell of garlic, which he detested. He urged each husband to give up smoking and avoid corrupting his wife's "sweet breath" and thereby deliver her from "a perpetuall stinking torment."

The King's denunciation concluded, thunderingly, with: "A custom loathsome to the eye, hateful to the nose, harmfull to the braine, dangerous to the lungs, and in the black stinking fume thereof, neerest resembling the horrible Stigian smoke of the pit that is bottomlesse."

Though James's pamphlet was widely read, consumption of tobacco from Virginia rose sharply. Frustrated by his fruitless attempts to suppress smoking, the King arranged a debate on the subject of smoking, to be held at Oxford University. On August 29, 1605, the King heard doctors and professors argue the pros and cons of the question, "Is the use of tobacco beneficial or not to a healthy man?" When fust and bombast subsided, the King delivered his own opinion, repeating the bitter remarks in his *Counter-blaste to Tobacco.*

Then up stepped one Dr. Cheynall to face the King with a lighted pipe in hand. Cheynall delivered a witty speech in defense of tobacco. The audience laughed. The moderator laughed. The King laughed. But at the end of the morning-long debate, the royal views prevailed. It seems extraordinary that the daring displayed by Dr. Cheynall, who must be regarded as one of pipe smoking's most courageous heroes, did not have serious consequences.

Sir Walter Raleigh, that earlier member of pipe smoking's hall of fame, was not so fortunate. King James disliked Raleigh because he smoked incessantly. His Royal Highness found an excuse to charge Raleigh with conspiracy and condemned him to death. Although Raleigh, founder of the Virginia colonies that were the home of tobacco, was reprieved on the scaffold, he was imprisoned in a dungeon in the Tower of London, where, according to historians, "he sorely missed his tobacco." Raleigh was released in 1617 and placed in command of a fleet that was to conquer the golden land of El Dorado. James ordered Raleigh to avoid any encounter with the Spaniards. Circumstances, however, forced Raleigh to do battle with them. When the smoke cleared, his own son lay dead. The King, however, had little sympathy for his pipe-smoking admiral. He signed a death warrant. If Raleigh did not have the last word, he did have the last gesture. Before going to the chopping block, he insisted on smoking one last pipe.

Meanwhile, the importation of tobacco from Virginia became a highly important industry. In Virginia, tobacco became legal tender. Ninety Virginia planters purchased English wives who were advertised as "agreeable persons, young and incorrupt." Cost of these importations: 120 pounds of tobacco. In 1621 the price went up: "Sixty maids of virtuous education, young and handsome" brought a record-breaking 150 pounds of tobacco apiece.

Back in London, apparently unmoved by the fierce opposition of their King, pipe makers formed a guild, incorporating under the motto "Let Brotherly Love Continue." Their shield, depicting a tobacco plant in bloom, must have set the monarch's teeth on edge whenever he had to pass beneath it. He continued to oppose and discourage the tobacco trade, but with scant success—despite the fact that he was not without support from several quarters. Austria, though caught in the tobacco contagion, in 1590 prohibited the use of tobacco. In 1596 anti-tobacconists seized upon the fact that the Bishop of London died "while sitting in his chair taking tobacco." A few years later another English enemy of the weed asserted "four people have died from tobacco within a week. One of them voided a bushel of soot." And in 1612, in faraway China, planting or use of tobacco was forbidden by Imperial edict.

Nevertheless, when James died in 1625 it was

said of London that "tobacco shops are in greater number than alehouses or taverns." James's son Charles, who succeeded him, was also a tobacco-phobe, pedantic and fanatical. Little anti-smoking progress was made in England, but during the next few years the fight picked up speed in other places. In 1634 the Russian Czar prohibited smoking, and decreed, "For first offense smokers shall be whipped; for the second, executed." In Greece the Church declared that tobacco fumes had intoxicated Noah, and issued an edict against smoking.

Civil War split England in 1642, pitting Charles and his pipe-loving Cavaliers against another non-smoker with a pipe-smoking army, Oliver Cromwell, commander of the Roundheads. Charles was captured and sentenced "to death by severing his Head from his Body." G. L. Apperson, in his *Social History of Smoking*, says that when the sentence had been read, "the soldiers treated the fallen monarch with great indignity and barbarity. They spat on his clothes as he passed by, and even in his face, and they blew 'the smoak of Tobacco, a thing which they knew His Majesty hated, in his sacred mouth, throwing their broken pipes in his way as he passed along.' "

Swiftly, the popularity of the pipe, fostered by the English, won over a continent that had for some time tried, and wearied of, snuff. That the pipe should triumph over the snuffbox is scarcely surprising when one reads these instructions on the rigmarole of snuff taking, published in an early pamphlet on smoking:

1. Take the snuff with your right hand.
2. Pass the snuff-box to your left hand.
3. Rap the snuff-box.
4. Open the snuff-box.
5. Present the box to the company.
6. Receive it after going the round.
7. Gather up the snuff in the box by striking the side with the middle and forefinger.
8. Take up a pinch with the right hand.
9. Keep the snuff a moment or two between the fingers before carrying it to the nose.
10. Put the snuff to your nose.
11. Sniff it in with precision by both nostrils and without any grimace.
12. Shut the snuff-box, sneeze, spit and wipe your nose.

The pipe spread throughout Europe by the same routes as tobacco itself. By 1600 nearly every Dutchman had his favorite clay. During epidemics, such as the plague of 1636, physicians urged the frightened Dutch to protect themselves by taking up their pipes. One physician, Isbrand von Diemerbrock, offers this vivid description of the conditions at plague-stricken Nimeguen:

> The people who always turn to their superiors for guidance, turned in plague time to the doctors for instructions on how to avoid the danger of infection. It was my habit at that time to smoke daily after each meal. . . . As I have proved by long experience, tobacco is the

most effective means of avoiding the plague—
provided the leaf is in good condition. One
day, when I was visiting one of the victims,
the reek of the pestilence seemed to overpower
me, and I felt all of the symptoms of infection
—dizziness, nausea, fear; I cut short my visit
and hurried home—where I smoked six or
seven pipes of tobacco. I was myself once
more. . . . Only once, when I was visiting a
married couple sick with the plague, I delayed
too long in trying my usual antidote, and
nearly lost my life in consequence; although I
smoked several pipes I felt so ill that I lay
down again and passed into a state of uncon-
sciousness. When some hours later my servant
woke me to say that a number of sick persons
were waiting for me I got up, and it was only
with my servant's help that I was able to reach
the fireplace where lay my pipe—but, after
smoking it, I made an instantaneous recovery.

All over Europe, claims for the pipe grew steadily. Dr. Hovey, Dr. Fowler, and other physicians
joined Diemerbrock in recommending the use of
tobacco during the plague. Papers and pamphlets
described tobacco as "an excellent defense against
bad air." One exuberant panegyrist, Dr. Thorious,
wrote that pipe smoke

cleanseth the air and choaketh and suppresseth
and disperseth any venemous vapour; it hath
both singular and contrary effects; it is good

to warm one being cold, and will cool one being hot; it giveth thirst and yet will make one more fit and able to take drink; it chokes hunger and yet will give one a good stomach; it is agreeable with mirth or sadness, with feasting and with fasting; it will make one rest that wants sleep, and will keep waking one that is drowsy; it hath an offensive smell, and is more desirable than perfume to others. . . .

But in addition to the medicinal properties claimed for it, the pipe was being celebrated, though not in so many words, for its psychological, social, and emotional attributes. Lord and lackey, peer and peasant, chimneysweep and chamberlain —all were learning that pipe smoking is an enormously satisfying thing to do. One philosopher of the day wrote, "If time hang heavy and he has nothing else to do, a man will [take] tobacco. If he is moody, angry or perplexed, he sticks his pipe between his teeth and takes a long pull at it. Should his wife begin to nag, the man will fill his mouth with smoke and puff it in her face."

One of the most impassioned pleas for tobacco was penned by one Henry James Meller, Esquire, who argued,

Smoking that is called unsocial, the author affirms to be the common source of harmony and comfort, the badge of good fellowship in almost every state, kingdom and empire—aye, from the English settlers in the wilderness of

America, where the Calumet or Pipe of Peace is smoked, to the turbaned infidel of the East ... smoking that is termed low and vulgar was, and is, an occasional recreation with most of the crowned heads of Europe ... smoking that is termed idle is singularly popular with mechanics, the most industrious classes of England ... smoking that is said to be dirty and filthy is in the greatest esteem among the most moral and cleanly sect in Christianity—the Society of Friends or Quakers ... smoking that is affirmed to be revolting and disgusting is indulged in by the most rigidly kept women in the world—those of Turkey who, elevated in the dignity of the Harem, are taught to consider a whiff of their lord's *chibouque* a distinction ... smoking that is called beastly is used to the greatest excess in the famed land of *politesse*—France.

As wars flickered and flared across the continent, tobacco—despite the unflagging opposition of hardcore detractors who were never won over—completed its conquest of civilization. During the period after the Thirty Years War, however, the pipe began to meet with effective resistance. Between 1649 and 1652, as a consequence of certain pointed inquiries on the part of Emperor Ferdinand III, use of tobacco was prohibited in Cologne, Bavaria, Munich, and Stuttgart. On May 19, 1653, this edict was addressed to the whole of Saxony:

Whereas the colonel of the fortress had given strict orders to his soldiers, as likewise the burgomaster to his citizens, that one and all should abstain from the deadly tobacco habit, and whereas such orders had been so little regarded that on April 25, through the carelessness of certain smokers, a fire had broken out in the cellar of the town hall of Dresden, be it known to all that for the future not only is smoking absolutely forbidden to soldiers and civilians alike, both in beer-houses and cellars, but tobacco must no longer be sold except in apothecaries' shops, as ordered by a doctor's prescription.

Despite such edicts, more and more people smoked more and more pipes. One report states that "there were some who would smoke 40, 50 and even more pipes a day." In Switzerland, too, the anti-tobacconists, led by the clergy, clamored for effective legislation to prohibit smoking. In Zurich, in 1667, an edict warned "the lazy, good-for-nothing crew" of smokers that they would be beaten with rods and branded if they continued to smoke. The Swiss National Assembly ordered stiff fines for smokers. The cantons of Berne, Lucerne, Unterwalden, Fribourg, and Soleure formed a coalition to stamp out the vice. Mayors, magistrates, clerics, counselors— all raised their voices against the "loathsome habit." Meanwhile, back at the chalet, Swiss menfolk, wreathed in smoke and smiles, introduced their servants, wives, and daughters to the joys of smoking.

Toward the end of the 17th century, Italy, long permissive with regard to smoking, adopted the official attitude of the rest of Europe. In Turkey the bloodthirsty Sultan Murad, who was crowned at the age of 14, forbade the use of tobacco under the penalty of death. The Sultan, known as Murad the Cruel, made a nocturnal practice of secretly visiting certain resorts. Any man unlucky enough to be observed smoking over his coffee was, unbeknownst to himself, enjoying his last night out—or anywhere. The next morning the smoker's body would be found in front of the resort, a grim reminder of the Sultan's determination to be heeded by his subjects.

According to one historian,

> Even French interpreters were impaled and hanged, while in the case of certain ambassadors from Persia, he [Murad] had their noses and ears cut off and sent the wretched victims away with their dispatches nailed to the gaping wounds thus made. Having given his own physician a fatal dose of opium, he made him sit down with him to a game of chess, in order better to watch and enjoy the sight of his struggle with death. . . . Even on the battlefield he was fond of surprising men in the act of smoking . . . he would punish them by beheading, hanging, quartering, or crushing their

hands and feet and leaving them helpless between the lines.

The prohibitions of Murad, however, like those
of other rulers, proved futile against the power of
tobacco. And in a short time the legislative pendu-
lum was to swing back toward the pro-tobacconists,
for governments had become aware of the fact that
enormous revenue could be realized through tobacco taxes. The Emperor Leopold of Austria, for
example, granted a tobacco monopoly to one of his
counts in order to finance a hunt in Upper Austria.
In 1674 Louis XIV announced a plan to raise
revenue from tobacco as a way "of making it easier
for our people to bear a part of the extraordinary
expenses of the present war." Everywhere, tobacco
prohibition was falling before the policy of tobacco
taxation.

In 1670 Charles II of England ordered all tobacco plants in England and Ireland destroyed, for
he had discovered that it was easier to control customs duty on imported Virginia tobacco. Swiftly
the tone of the literature of the day changed from
one of hostility toward tobacco to one of nearly
boundless enthusiasm. In the comedy *Don Juan*,
Molière, the great French playwright, had a poet
say,

> Whatever Aristotle and all the philosophers
> may say, there is nothing like tobacco; it is the
> passion of all proper people, and he who lives
> without tobacco has nothing to live for. Not

only does it refresh and cleanse men's brains, but it guides their souls in the ways of virtue, and by it one learns to be a man of honour. Do you not see how readily men offer their tobacco right and left, wherever they are? No one waits to be asked; he anticipates another's wish; so true is it that tobacco begets honourable and virtuous sentiments in all those who use it.

What Molière said, Corneille said better when he versified Molière's comedy:

Whatever Aristotle's school declare,
Tobacco is divine, beyond compare,
And to employ aright an idler's leisure,
No sport is there that gives so great a pleasure.

Louis XIV did not share the views of the poets and philosophers who prattled and prated the praises of tobacco. He hated the weed. Nevertheless, except for a critical minority, the members of his court smoked like chimneys when their monarch was not about. The Princess Palatine Liselotte, wife of Philip of Orleans, the King's brother, wrote, "All the women in Paris go stripped (i.e., with neck and bosom bare) and it disgusts me—you can see almost down to their waists . . . they all look as if they were just out of a madhouse . . . the women are too contemptible with their dress, their drinking, their tobacco which makes them smell horribly."

By the 18th century there were few Liselottes to

carp about smoking. Everyone smoked. Middle-sized Dutch clay pipes were the mode among the middle and lower classes, with delicate china pipes the fashion in high society. But evidently the universality of the habit diminished its chic, despite the class line drawn by the china pipe. Snuff regained its popularity and presented a dangerous challenge to the pipe. In aristocratic circles, smoking became *déclassé* and snuff once more *de rigueur*.

In Germany, however, the pipe continued to hold sway for a long time because, one may assume, the nobility followed the example of the first two kings of Prussia, Frederick I and Frederick William I, both enthusiastic pipesters. Both held tobacco parties, and Frederick William formed a tobacco club that met daily. Count Corti writes,

At the Tobacco Club, everyone had merely beer and a short Dutch clay pipe of the common kind; the King alone had a silver-mounted pipe. The tobacco, Dutch leaf, was on the table in wicker baskets, with little pans of glowing peat to light the pipes. The servants, when the room was ready, were sent away and forbidden to enter the room till the Club meeting was over, so that members could talk freely and crack jokes to their heart's content . . . but the chief business of the meeting was smoking, and the King sometimes—especially when his friend Stanislaus, the ex-King of Poland, was there—smoked all night. In 1735, they used to smoke 30 pipes and more from five in the afternoon to two o'clock next morning. . . . It was torment for members of this society who did not smoke to sit in a cloud of smoke. The Old Dessauer [Field Marshal Leopold I, Prince of Anhalt-Dessau], who could never bring himself to smoke, sat among the guests with an unlighted pipe in his mouth, and by his side Count Seckendorf, the Imperial Ambassador. . . . Both of them, in order to satisfy the rules of the Club, puffed away like thorough smokers.

Nevertheless, snuff taking continued to increase in other European countries. Its popularity was partially due to the fact that, in cities built almost entirely of wood, pipes constituted a fire hazard. The safety aspect of snuff, which did not require flint, steel, and tinder, appealed to many. Also, snuff was considered by women to be the more genteel of the two habits. But in 1715 one Mme. Leucorande spoke up for the pipe. She contended that a pipe promotes longevity and took it upon herself to write a little book with the large title, *A Sound and Pleasant Proof that a Respectable Woman may sometimes enter a Coffee-house without Damage to her Good Name, and moreover she may, and should, treat herself to a Pipe of Tobacco. Further, it is also explained why Women go first, and why Men wear Beards. All most briefly and pleasantly proved, and maintained by Incontestable Reasons.*
Her views found many supporters. One, Dr. J. J. W. Beintema, wrote, ". . . it is a glorious venture

when a woman takes heart to smoke a pipe of tobacco. Her charming sex has an equal right to
men." History also relates the anecdote of a girl
who asked that tobacco be planted over her grave
"that the weed nourished by her dust might be
chewed by her bereaved lovers." The anecdote
prompted an early-day Charles Addams to suggest
this epitaph:

> *Let no cold marble o'er my body rise—*
> *But only earth above and sunny skies.*
> *Thus would I lowly lie in peaceful rest,*
> *Nursing the Herb Divine from out my breast.*
> *Green let it grow above this clay of mine,*
> *Deriving strength from strength that I resign.*
> *So in the days to come, when I'm beyond*
> *This fickle life, will come my lovers fond,*
> *And gazing on the plant, their grief restrain*
> *In whispering, "Lo! dear Anna blooms again!"*

On every hand, the prohibitions against smoking
were being discarded. Pope Benedict XIII, who was
fond of smoking, repealed an order that threatened
persons who smoked in church with immediate ex-
communication. Impartially, he also permitted both
clergy and laity to enjoy snuff taking in the very
center of the Catholic Church—St. Peter's.

For a time, snuff taking grew so rapidly that it
seemed smoking was doomed to extinction, but a
new form of smoking was to come along and de-
throne the snuffbox favored in royal circles. The
villain—or hero, depending on one's viewpoint—
was the cigar.

Even as Europeans lit their first cigars, a fuse that had been burning for some time burst into flame, igniting the French Revolution and plunging Europe into a war that was to rage almost continuously for a quarter of a century. As the sale of tobacco had appealed to Benjamin Franklin as a means for the United States to finance its War of Independence, so, too, did tobacco appeal to Napoleon as a source of revenue. He passed strict economic measures that affected every smoker. The story goes that the economic significance of tobacco was brought home to Napoleon when he admired the jewels of a passing woman. Upon being told that her husband was a tobacco merchant, he promptly raised tobacco prices to reap more money for his war machine.

Napoleon himself, though a prodigious snuff taker, had little use for pipe smoking. According to one anecdote, an Ambassador from Persia persuaded him to try a richly ornamented waterpipe. The smoke went down the wrong way. When the upstart Bonaparte recovered from a violent fit of coughing, he cried, "Take it away! How foul! You pigs, it makes me sick."

Despite Napoleon's disenchantment with the pipe, smokers abounded in his Grande Armee. It is said of LaSalle that he led cavalry charges with his pipe clenched in his teeth and made a special point of capturing a field marshal who owned a prized meerschaum. Mortally wounded at the battle of Essling, Jean Lannes stoically puffed a pipe while surgeons amputated both his legs.

Speaking of the popularity of the pipe among Napoleon's soldiers, one writer asserts, "While the army's march was daily and nightly strewed with the dead and the dying, and many a gallant fellow breathed his last on the cold beds of snow, they were wonderfully sustained by their pipes, which kept up their spirits throughout the scene of famine and desolation."

One report from the front, which could almost have been written by a correspondent named Bill Mauldin, stated:

> When the maimed and shattered lie upon the sodden battlefield, what do they most piteously cry for? Tobacco! In the hospitals, where are found the wounded—poor, useless wrecks of a-day-before's glorious humanity— what is supplied to them so liberally and is more essential to those apparent bundles of lint and splinters than medicine? Tobacco! In the heat of battle, when coolness is the most desirable of all soldierly qualities, what are the best marksmen doing? Smoking! As the smoke of their powder reeks from their heated rifles, the thin smoke of tobacco curls from their lips.

As if that were not enough to put in one's pipe to smoke, there is also this anecdote from the front. The dialogue is offered as that of a soldier and his officer upon the battlefield.

SOLDIER: Och, murther, I'm kilt entirely.

OFFICER: Are you wounded?

SOLDIER: Wounded is it, yer honour? Be the powers, I'm worse than kilt out an' out! Wasn't I waitin' for the last quarter of an hour for a pull of Jim Murphy's pipe? An' there, now, it's shot out of his mouth!

Although the war that flamed across Europe made tobacco harder to get, it ignited an increasing number of pipes and cigars in every country. Many new cigar factories were built—so many that the cigar threatened to eclipse both snuffbox and pipe. That the pipe managed to hold its ground at all may be explained in part by the fact that pipes had acquired a dimension forever denied to cigars—the status of art. Many pipes were designed by such noted artists as Wedgwood. Pipes also owed a debt of gratitude to the cigar for stamping out the snuffbox. Too, there was a safety factor involved. Cigars were thought to be more dangerous than pipes. At the court of Windsor, for example, smokers had to puff their cigars in front of the fireplace so that the smoke would go up the chimney.

Germany was among the last of the European nations to sink its teeth into the cigar. Describing the novelty in his *Konversationslexicon*, Brockhaus wrote, in 1809,

We must mention here a new style of smoking, namely *cigarros;* these are tobacco leaves rolled into hollow cylinders of the thickness of

a finger. One end is lighted and the other put
in the mouth. This is how they are smoked.
This method, which is used in Spanish America
instead of the pipe, is beginning to be common
in our parts also; but whether it makes tobacco taste better or no is hard to determine,
for it is—a mere question of taste.

With the advance of the cigar, pipe smoking and
snuff taking continued to decline. But after the
Crimean War in 1856 a new discovery rivalled,
then surpassed, the cigar. Called *papelitos* in Brazil,
the new smoke was the now-familiar cigarette, well
known to South America in the 18th century and
described in the memoirs of Casanova as follows:
"The good fellow was carelessly puffing at his cigarette of Brazilian tobacco wrapped in a little paper
tube from which he blew great clouds of smoke
with evident enjoyment."

Slowly the cigarette won acclaim, first in Spain,
then in France and Italy. Napoleon III, compensat-
ing for his ancestor's hatred of smoking, became
addicted to the convenient little tube. It is said that,
viewing the carnage of the Battle of Solferino, he
muttered, "Poor creatures, what a terrible thing is
war!" and solaced himself by chain-smoking. The
"paper cigar," as it was called by one manufacturer,
offered one decisive advantage over the cigar. The
cost of rolling a cigarette was but a fraction of the
cost of purchasing a ready-made cigar. Nonetheless,
early ready-made cigarettes did meet with opposition. For one thing, they were made of cheap paper

and often contained inferior tobacco. Queen Victoria, always an enemy of tobacco, on one occasion turned round and issued a sharp reprimand to those who adulterated it with dyes, alum, saltpeter, bran, meals, sawdust, muscatel, peat earth, and leaves. And those who smoked cigarettes were often branded dandies and fops.

When finer tobacco and paper were employed in its manufacture, the cigarette became of age. Almost overnight, in England and North America, cigarettes became the preferred smoke of Everyman. As might be expected, the cigarette's slowest progress was made in cigar-loving Germany.

More curious is the fact that the cigarette, though developed in South America, did not reach North America until it had become fashionable in Europe. As recently as the Civil War, the cigar enjoyed greater popularity in this country than the cigarette. When, in 1862, General Ulysses S. Grant captured Fort Donelson, the grateful Union presented him with a gift of 11,000 cigars. By 1904, when three large firms merged to form The American Tobacco Company, the big guns of the American tobacco industry were well under way. Like the pipe, snuffbox, and cigar before it, the cigarette made enemies. Tolstoy, it is said, spent much of his life as an avowed enemy of smoking. Henry Ford was a fanatical tobaccophobe and, had it been possible, would have insisted that all of his employees give up cigarettes. These crusaders would have found modern medical ammunition in the Surgeon General's report, discussed in Chapter 2.

Yet the chances are that even with such ammunition they would not have achieved their goal. Throughout history the question "To smoke or not smoke?" has been, in every way, a burning issue. Yet every organized effort to stamp out smoking has been unsuccessful. Man being a perverse creature, and history a saga that retells itself, it seems unlikely that taxes, wars, medical testimony, or legislation will ever succeed in parting him from the herb that has been his boon companion for thousands of years.

In particular, it appears that the pipe will survive. Whether or not the growing torrent of medical evidence succeeds in extinguishing the popularity of the cigarette—and in the light of current sales figures this seems unlikely—the pipe, which has been with us since the dawn of smoking, promises to go on forever, and is even now enjoying a revival that suggests that a Golden Age of Pipe Smoking is here.

CHAPTER 5

MANY KINDS OF PIPES

THE PIPE has outlived snuff and survived its threatened eclipse by cigar and cigarette for a number of reasons, but the primary one is simple: it is the most attractive, most effective means yet devised by which the smoker can obtain full pleasure from tobacco.

As we have seen, the idea of breathing in smoke *through* something occurred to the first men who adapted hollow reeds for the purpose. Since then, man has contrived to make pipes out of nearly every substance that can be bored or pierced—bone and stone, lobster claw and seashell, coconut and conch. Artists have contributed further stature to these objects, fashioning pipes that were possessed of a beauty as eternal and immutable as the simple principle of the bowl and the mouthpiece. Most pipe smokers believe that these artistic efforts culminated in the briar, which is discussed in the following chapter, and find that there is nothing in pipe history, past or current, to surpass it; but the fact remains that the experimental smoker or the collector can find scores of nonbriar pipes on the market whose novel features make them worthy of attention—among them chibouk, narghile, gambier, porcelain, calabash, corncob, churchwarden, and meerschaum.

In appearance, the *chibouk* (which means *wand* or *stick* in Turkish) is among the most distinctive of pipes. Two to three feet long, the stem gives way to a bell-shaped bowl that is usually made of red clay. Brightly colored cords decorate the long stem and reinforce the sections of pipe where they are joined. At the base of the pipe there are often several apertures into which additional stems may be placed, thereby making the chibouk a most sociable pipe. The *imaneh*, or mouthpiece, of the chibouk is usually made of tortoise shell or amber, though sometimes bone is used.

It seems likely that the chibouk and similar pipes were inspired by the Indian peace pipe, called the calumet by the French. The literature on such pipes is as fascinating as it is extensive, as evidenced by the very thorough book, *Pipes and Smoking Customs of the American Aborigines*, written by Joseph D. McGuire in 1898. The stem of the calumet is usually about four feet long and decorated with the feathers of the great owl and war eagle, colored horsehair, white rabbit fur, and porcupine quills, though the symbolic decorations varied from tribe to tribe. Being cumbersome, the pipe was often placed upon a forked support when it was smoked.

McGuire states, "The friendly offering of the pipe is evidently an ancient custom and one referred to by many of the earliest visitors to the Atlantic coast, though in council the pipe does not appear to have been so prominent an adjunct in the East as it was in the Valley of the Mississippi, where in all functions between the French and the natives the calumet occupied an important position."

Used chiefly to negotiate treaties, the pipes were held dear. Among the Crees, for example, a man had to pay from 15 to 20 horses for the honor of carrying the pipe of ceremony. Some tribes, such as the Kiowas and Sioux, had, in addition to peace pipes, highly decorated tomahawk pipes. McGuire laments, "It is to be regretted that the history of the tomahawk pipe is so incomplete in American writings, for it certainly has occupied as important a place, both in war and peace, over a great part of the continent as any pipe known, and is peculiarly a war pipe and one of the most familiar and terrible weapons of the allies of the whites in the endless colonial wars of America."

The weapon was in the form of a spear or hatchet head on one side with a cup-like cavity— the pipe bowl—on the other. A hole, bored at a right angle below the hollow of the bowl, provided for the insertion of the pipe stem. Although tomahawk pipes are now precious collectors' items, many good imitations of the calumet, or peace pipe, are on the market. To the pipe hobbyist, the calumet, authentic or simulated, affords a colorful conversation piece and an occasional cool smoke.

For what appears to be a Rube Goldberg contraption, turn to the *narghile*, a water pipe that is related to the chibouk and is popular with the Turks and Asians. Persians, Dutch, English—all claim to have invented the water pipe, but a considerable case can be advanced for the pygmies and bushmen of Africa, who used sections of bamboo and water-filled gourds to smoke hemp. Coconuts were also used, being tough, durable, and easy to hollow out, and, indeed, the Indian word *narghile* means "coco-nut-shell." Called *hookah* by the Turkish and *kalian* by the Persians, the water pipe consists of a glass bowl that holds water—sometimes scented—and two tubes. One tube conveys the smoke from the burning tobacco to the sealed water chamber; the other enables the smoker to draw the smoke through the water. One early writer on the subject of Persian smoking habits states, "The excessive use of the pipe dries up the Persians and weakens them. They admit this fact, but when asked why they do not quit the habit, reply, 'There is no joy for the heart except by tobacco!'"

In point of fact, the narghile offers the coolest, mildest smoke of any pipe, and in terms of design and ornamentation often constitutes a genuine work of art. If the tubes, wrapped in gaily colored silk with a proliferation of tassels, are not enough to titillate one's imagination, it may be remembered that narghiles are also used for smoking a large variety of narcotics, including opium.

A truly stupendous description of the proper setting for smoking a narghile occurs in a 19th-century tract titled, *A Peep into the Harem:*

> A fair idea of the importance attached to smoking by Turkish women of high rank may be obtained by a visit to the Harem of the

Khedive of Egypt at the Ismailia Palace on the banks of the Nile. The audience chamber of His Highness's only wife is a casket fit for a jewel. The furniture is of ivory and mother-of-pearl, and the hangings of silvery satins, embroided with pale roses and violets in silk and silver thread. The ceiling and woodwork are painted with groups of flowers . . . while the floor is covered with thick Aubusson rugs strewn with a design of rose leaves and buds. Here, lying back on a low divan, is the Queen, clothed in white silken tissues cut a l'Europienne with a great profusion of marvelous lace and a perfect shower of pearls and diamonds glittering in her hair . . . (and) her slippers thickly sewn with brilliants.

On her heart she wears a miniature of her husband framed with huge diamonds and rubies and around her waist is a broad band of the same stones to which is suspended a fan of snowy ostrich feathers, its handle encrusted with pearls, emeralds and sapphires.

The author notes that "in spite of all this, there is nothing discordant in the sovereign's appearance," and then goes on to describe the Queen's narghile pipe: "The bowl is of engraved rock crystal mounted in chased gold, fashioned in the form of a lotus flower. The tube is concealed by a deftly wrought network of pink silk and gold thread while the amber mouthpiece and gold plateau are one mass of sparkling jewels."

In many parts of the world today, the clay pipe retains a sizeable following. One of the best-known forms is the gambier, named after its inventor. Though the bowl may be shaped like a head, the more familiar gambier has strikingly clean lines, broken only by the small knob beneath the bowl that allows the smoker to hold the hot pipe. Gambiers suffer the disadvantage of being extremely breakable. As a consequence, they cannot be considered portable, though this is less true of the gambiers with cherrywood stems or those that have ebonite mouthpieces affixed to the pipe with a metal ring.

From a historical view, the clay pipe is a deposed king. The plain clay known as the "cutty" and the longer, gracefully curved churchwarden were once the biggest selling pipes in England. Apperson writes in his *Social History of Smoking*, "In the 'fifties the pipes smoked were mostly clays. There were the long clays or 'churchwardens,' to be smoked in hours of ease and leisure; and the short clays—'cutties'—which could be smoked while a man was at work." Milo, a tobacconist in the Strand, and Inderwick, whose shop was near Leicester Square, were famous for their pipes, which could be bought for 6d. apiece. A burlesque poem of 1853, in praise of an old black pipe, says

> *Think not of meerschaum is that bowl: away,*
> *Ye fond enthusiasts! It is common clay,*
> *By Milo stamped, perchance by Milo's hand,*
> *And for a tizzy purchased in the Strand.*

In a pamphlet printed in 1891, it is said of the clay that "a cutty bowl, like a Creole's eye, is most prized when blackest." As a rule, however, it takes the clay pipe some time to turn black.

The chief advantage of the clay pipe was that it was very inexpensive. Often it was thrown away after one smoke. On the other hand, clay pipes smoke "strong." The taste is rough, earthy, and has been known to rock the novice back on his heels. Still, devotees of clays are as eager to rhapsodize as the poets of the briar and the meerschaum. Of a broken clay pipe, James Thomson wrote

> *Neglected now it lies, a cold clay form,*
> *So late with living inspirations warm:*
> *Type of all other creatures formed of clay—*
> *What more than it for Epitaph have they?*

The fact that the factories in Gouda, Holland, a city as famous for its clay pipes as its cheeses, still turn out some 7,000,000 pipes a year is proof of the continued popularity of the clay pipe. Production, however, is but a small fraction of what it was before the briar pipe brought the luxury of owning a fine, durable pipe within financial reach of Everyman.

There are still porcelain pipes on the market. But like clays, porcelain pipes attain such a high temperature that they must be equipped with a knob or similar device. The beard on the pipes sculpted to depict Jacob, for example, is intended to protect the smoker's hand from the hot bowl.

Save for their often spectacular designs and dimen-
sions—some hold as much as two ounces of tobacco
—there seems little to recommend the porcelains,
once so popular in Germany and France. For one
thing, these pipes often split or crack on the very
first smoking. Also, the highly ornamented porcelains, especially the Alsatians so much sought after
by romantic tourists, frequently tend to collect
nicotine and other disagreeable juices in such quantity as to smell like a chamberpot in need of emptying. But by way of balancing this unfortunate characteristic, porcelains, like meerschaums, can—if one
is lucky or skillful—acquire a beautiful coloring. In
Germany, where the porcelain pipe was once considered almost a national symbol, students often
had their pipes decorated with the emblems of their
secret societies.

Among the novel pipes, the calabash is easily the
most aristocratic, bringing to mind the image of
Sherlock Holmes, pipe in mouth and magnifying
glass in hand, peering from beneath his deerstalk-
er's cap. The calabash is the neck of a gourd fitted
with a meerschaum bowl. The cultivation of the
gourd is ingenious, for its neck is trained to grow
to the desired shape. Despite such rigid control,
each gourd differs slightly from the others, reflect-
ing the whims and caprices of Nature. As a consequence, no two calabashes are exactly alike, leading
one to speculate that the calabash is the ultimate
pipe for status seekers. Besides being unique, the
graceful calabash is among the lightest of pipes, for
after the gourd has been dried and hollowed it

weighs next to nothing. The meerschaum insert is also quite light and is fitted into the gourd with a featherweight cork gasket. For reading or fireside philosophizing, the calabash has few peers—and the added advantage of coloring well.

Of Senators Thurman and Edmunds, who were very good friends, poet Albert Pike wrote

> *Not from cigars the Senate stars*
> *Their inspiration drew;*
> *Old pipes they smoked, as they sat and joked—*
> *Yes, pipes, and cob pipes too!*

The roster of men who inclined toward a corncob is a distinguished one, and includes Daniel Boone and General Douglas MacArthur. Mark Twain is reputed to have done much of his writing while puffing on a corncob, and it has been said that he hired a man to break in new ones.

The capital of corncob country is Washington, Missouri, where upwards of 15,000,000 "Missouri meerschaums" are manufactured every year. Almost without exception, the pipes are made from the big, rugged cobs of "Collier" corn, a slow-growing, tall-standing strain. After the cobs have been harvested, by which time they are more than two inches in diameter, they are shelled, sorted, and put aside to dry—often for as long as two years. Machines smooth the cobs and bore the bowls. When soft spots in the cob have been reinforced with plaster, the pipe is fitted with a stem, varnished, labeled, and sent to market.

To obtain the most pleasure from a corncob pipe, the smoker should smoke slowly and have several pipes to rotate so that each pipe will have a chance to dry thoroughly. Since the days of the Indians, believed by some historians to have been the first men to smoke the cob, the lowly Missouri meerschaum has steadily gained in popularity.

Other pipes available to the collector include the Moorish pipe of mutton bone which yields only five or six puffs of smoke, the asbestos pipe made in Dublin shapes, the earthenware "Elfin" and "Fairy" pipes that continue to turn up in Scotland and Ireland, and a staggering variety of African pipes, some as cumbersome and complicated as a contrabassoon.

But these are all novelties. The active smoker who is neither a clay nor a briar man is almost certain to be a member of the meerschaum faction.

If the briar is the King of pipes, then meerschaum is surely Queen. True meerschaum, a mineral with unique properties, comes almost exclusively from Turkey. It is believed that the first lump of meerschaum to be carved into a pipe was presented to Count Andrassy of Austria in 1723. A heavy smoker, Andrassy noted that the gift was light and porous, an ideal substance from which to carve a pipe. Returning to Pesth (now Budapest, Hungary), the Count gave the strange white substance to a shoemaker who was also an excellent carver.

The cobbler, Karl Kowates, made two pipes. The first he gave to the count. The second he kept. When he had smoked it once, he noticed that the bowl had turned a golden brown where his wax-stained fingers had touched it. To correct the blotchy appearance of his pipe, the cobbler coated the rest of the bowl with wax and lighted up again. Gradually, the bowl turned that rich nut-brown color that later prompted poet Francis Jammes to say of his own meerschaum, "I smoke a pipe as brown as the breast of a little negress." Exploiting his discovery, Kowates (referred to as Kovacs in some accounts) could not cope with the demand for his pipes. His original meerschaum is now prominently displayed in the national museum of his country.

For at least a century, the meerschaum was to be the hallmark of the very rich. During the 1800's, however, Austrian factories, in response to the discovery of new meerschaum deposits, turned out thousands of the pipes. Their popularity was universal. Poets, philosophers, pudding makers, and peasants all praised the delicate pipes.

In a smoker's guide published in 1877, the meerschaum is praised thus:

A perfect meerschaum pipe is decidedly one of the choicest and rarest gifts of the gods; but like all choice and rare gifts, it is a source of considerable anxiety to the owner. Like women, its "name is frailty." As originally taken in hand, and presented to the lips, nothing can exceed the loveliness of its looks—its delicious smoothness, its graceful rotundity of form, and apparent innocence from everything that can tarnish a reputation. But, alas! you take it as you take a wife, "for better or for worse"; and again, alas! it does not fare better with the smoker and his meerschaum than with man and wife. And the process of disenchantment, disappointment, and despair is pretty similar in both cases—it begins almost immediately. You find you are "in for it," and must "make the most of a bad bargain," if you are philosopher; if not (and here fortunately the comparison favours the smoker), you must "put it away," and get another.

It must be admitted that nothing can exceed the sweetness of an old meerschaum that was originally good and has been well-treated—to say nothing of its rich tint, indicative of its "blood"; but in light common use it always becomes encrusted with a hard and scaly residue of combustion, which, if not removed, rapidly diminishes the diameter of the bowl. This characteristic shows its imperfect absorption, the essential quality of a pipe. The burr is also detrimental to a very great extent, since it further prevents absorption.

Nevertheless, happy is the man to whom a good meerschaum has been vouchsafed! He should cherish it as a great blessing and not overwork it when it has become ambrosial, the quality described earlier in the discussion of the perfection of its savor and beauty of tint. The dying Gavarni said to his friend, "I consign my wife to your care, but oh, do take care of my *pipe*."

The unique coloration properties of meerschaum have produced enough purple poetry to fill all the tobacco pouches in the world. The prosecution offers these stanzas from a poem by Charles Loomis:

Speaking of color—do you know
A maid with eyes as darkly splendid
As are the hues that, rich and slow
On this Hungarian bowl have blended?

And this silver patched affair?
Well, sir, that meerschaum has its reasons
For showing marks of time and wear;
For in its smoke through fifty seasons

My grandsire blew his cares away!
And then, when done with life's sojourning,
At seventy-five dropped dead one day,
That pipe between his set teeth burning.

Loomis has a rival in one W. E. H., who, in 1875, penned this perfervid stanza to his meerschaum:

My Meerschaum Pipe is exquisitely dipped!
Shining, and silver-toned, and amber-tipped,
In close chromatic passages that number
The tones of brown from cinnamon to Um-
ber . . .

The very word *meerschaum* is poetically employed; it means, in German, "sea surf" and was used because the porous substance was originally thought to be petrified foam. The modern chemist's analysis is less poetic. Meerschaum is $H_4 Mg_2 Si_3 O_{10}$ or hydrous magnesium silicate, believed to be a metamorphosed sedimentary rock occurring in strata composed in part of seashells that fused together over a period of many aeons.

Meerschaum pipes are exceedingly difficult to manufacture. The first step is the mining of meerschaum. If the deposit lies close to the surface, a pick is used. Otherwise large open pits are dug. With special tools workmen remove clay from the "stones," which are then sanded, hewn into blocks, cut, turned, rubbed, polished, waxed, repolished, glazed, and, finally, finished.

This procedure, however, is true only of the fine meerschaum pipes cut directly from blocks. Pipes of inferior quality are made of a variety of clays, as well as certain synthetic materials. The French pipe expert E. Clerc wrote in 1866 that all pipes may be categorized as either "nonabsorbent" or capable of being impregnated, hence "absorbent." He expressed nothing but contempt for such nonabsorbent pipes as those made of porcelain, metal, wood—even briar—and called them mere contrivances for burning tobacco, stating that meerschaum alone liberates all of the elusive flavors and aromas. Although he admits, even in his lyrical enthusiasm, that the meerschaum is "fragile and terribly costly," he quickly adds that

    . . . no shadow can in any way be cast upon its merits. These merits are both exterior and interior. Exteriorly, of all pipes, meerschaum alone has the faculty of mellowing into a truly marvelous range of colors. These hues progress from a golden white to a rich brown, passing through the delicate pink of a china rose, a faint yellow, a golden yellow, pale orange, pinky brown, a light leather brown, warm brown, red brown, dark brown to an eventual black.

It is, of course, the immediate goal of every meerschaum smoker to bring out the color of his pipe as swiftly as possible. If the manufacturer has had the pipe boiled in beeswax, which is usually the case, the miracle will, indeed, quickly come to pass. On the fourth or fifth smoke, the meerschaum will respond in terms of color and flavor, assuming, of course, that the smoker has sedulously followed the manufacturer's instructions for breaking in the pipe.

In his affable *Social History of Smoking*, Apperson suggests that the earliest mention of the use of a wooden pipe was in 1765. He quotes a letter from Smollett who, in March of 1765, met a Quixotic figure atop Mt. Brovis: ". . . very tall, meagre and yellow with a long hooked nose and twinkling eyes. His head was cased in a woolen nightcap, over which he wore a flapped hat; he had a silk handkerchief about his neck, and his mouth was furnished with a short wooden pipe from which he discharged wreathing clouds of tobacco-smoke."

This encounter, according to Apperson, led a

Norfolk squire to try manufacturing pipes from willow wood. Says Apperson, "This experiment in the direction of wooden pipes was interesting and deserves to be remembered; but it was not long before the briar was introduced and carried everything before it."

It is certain that the briar has no equal. But the "experiment in the direction of wooden pipes" did lead to the limited use of other woods in pipe making. Of those available today, only two deserve discussion.

One is the rosewood pipe. Hailing from the West Indies, rosewood pipes offer a delicate taste that has been described by one enthusiastic writer as "hypnotic" and "soporific." These may be overstatements, but it is nonetheless true that rosewood does impart its unique and subtle bouquet to any blend of tobacco.

Known as *palissandre* in French, the wood of the Brazilian rosetree is medium-hard and usually of a deep, warm, brown color. Generally speaking, the pipes are made without mouthpieces but, in the interests of hygiene and of safeguarding the stem from unsightly teethmarks, the pipes may be fitted with an ebonite mouthpiece, adapted to the pipe with a metal band.

Caution: These pipes burn hot. When shopping for one, insist that the pipe have a butt or knob below the bowl like the one to be found on a clay or porcelain pipe.

For rustic charm, the cherrywood pipe, which always wears its original bark, has few peers. Like rosewood, it imparts its own flavor to the tobacco. But unlike rosewood, the cherrywood pipe is a big, robust fellow—usually, the bigger the better. The bowls are turned and hollowed from seasoned blocks of cherry and fitted with a stem. Costlier pipes utilize for a stem a branch growing out of the trunk. Besides being decorative, the bark discourages the bowl from cracking and splitting. Because cherrywood is inclined to char and burn, it should be smoked slowly—especially outdoors, where the wind is inclined to stimulate combustion. It is also helpful to pack the pipe somewhat more loosely than, say, a briar pipe.

Other woods used for pipe making and native to the U.S. include switch sorrel, wild lilac, and manzanita. Italian olive wood, African ebony, and American birch, hickory, maple, red gum, and a variety of fruitwoods other than cherry are among the nonburl woods that can, under certain conditions, provide creditable smoking.

It may be that it was the great variety of pipes on the market that moved one philosopher to paraphrase: "I often wonder what tobacconists buy one half so precious as the things they sell." A true pipester may have in his collection some, or all, of these fascinating types. But we see that most meerschaums, one of the three most-smoked pipes on the market, are expensive, and good. Most clays are inexpensive—and disappointing, if not downright disgusting, until pipe and smoker have had time to season one another. Thus it is that when the smoker lights up, the chances are 100 to 1 that he will have a briar between his teeth.

The disadvantage of briars is that they come in a bewildering array of sizes, shapes, and prices and offer a baffling variety of features. To the determined man this disadvantage becomes a challenge. A little time invested in research will insure against mistakes and pave an educated road to happy briarship.

CHAPTER 6

THE KING
OF PIPES

RETURNING TO APPERSON's *Social History of Smoking*, we find this note: "It was about 1859 that the use of the root of the White Heath (*Erica Arborea*), a native of the south of France, Corsica, and some other localities, for the purpose of making tobacco-pipes, was introduced into this country." The date is significant, for there is no question that from that time on the overwhelming choice of modern pipe smokers has been the briar.

Rugged, durable, very nearly fireproof, and boasting a handsome grain and a finish that often improves with age, the briar is deservedly titled the King of Pipes. It is not known who crowned His Majesty Briarwood, but there is reason to believe that no less exalted a figure than Napoleon III was, in a sense, responsible for the popularization of the briar. According to one historian, the briar was discovered in the 1850's by a French pipe maker, while making a pilgrimage to Napoleon's birthplace, Corsica.

The story goes that the pipe maker broke his meerschaum and sought a replacement for the pipe. He commissioned a peasant to carve a pipe from a wood famous locally for its hardness and fine grain. The briar proved *tout a fait magnifique*, and the Frenchman encouraged a factory at St. Claude to manufacture pipes of the French wood that is still regarded as the most successful pipe material ever discovered.

The story of an obscure pipe maker breaking his pipe while paying homage to the Little Corporal who was a victim of the disasters of 1814 is a touching tale but, in this writer's opinion, suspect. That a professional pipe maker would journey such a distance with only one meerschaum seems as unlikely as that Arnold Palmer would travel to Saint Andrews with but a single golfball in his bag.

Despite the similar name, briar pipes have no connection with the prickly, thorny briar that is often seen in hedgerows and that bears the lovely— but to smokers irrelevant—wild rose. As Apperson states, it is from the wood of the white heath—the French *bruyère*—that the briar pipe is fashioned. In fact, the first briar pipes were called bruyère or bruyer; as recently as February, 1868, according to the Oxford Dictionary, the *Tobacco Trade Review* advertised "Heath Pipe: in Bruyer Wood." However it is spelled, the briar pipe—hard, handsome, reasonably inexpensive, and tough—drove the clay pipe largely out of use and greatly increased the number of pipe smokers.

The heath tree, from the root of which briars are made, is a robust tree, dwarflike in appearance, that seldom exceeds a height of 25 feet. Requiring good soil and generous rainfall, it flourishes in parts of France, Corsica, Italy, and other Mediterranean countries. Paradoxically, the best briar comes from the areas least suited to its cultivation. On rock-strewn deserts, atop arid mountains, and in such bouldered woodlands as those found in Sardinia, where the heath tree must battle for its life, the bush, or knob at the confluence of the tree's roots, attains the toughest, tightest grain. In contrast, where idyllic conditions exist, the heath tree will pour its energies into luxuriant foliage at the expense of the burl that is used for pipe making.

For an exceedingly fine burl to develop, the growing period may be as long as 100 years or, in the case of truly exceptional specimens, two or three centuries. Because briar ages slowly, it has proved easier to find natural briar than to raise it commercially. A boon to modern pipe makers has been the recent exploitation of virgin briar forests in Greece, many of which are 100 years old.

Selection of briar by the pipesmith is an exacting matter. The burl must be very dry and hard. If a tiny stone or other foreign matter is embedded in the burl, it must be removed by the craftsman. This done, the briar is cut into rough shapes—large or small, round or oval, curved or straight. The briar is then steamed or boiled for several hours. Besides preventing splitting and cracking, the hot bath forces the briar to exude its sap. The pipes are then subjected to slow air drying—a tricky process, for the presence of a single draft of cold air can cause hundreds of briars to crack. The rough briar shapes are then sorted by size; the larger pieces are set aside for pipes with big bowls and the smaller ones for smaller bowls. The briars are then shaped on lathes, though the monks of St. Claude were famous for the skill with which they hand-carved each and every briar pipe. After being lathe-turned, the shanks of the pipes are drilled and the bowls are sandpapered to perfection.

Of every one hundred pipes, only one can be said to be perfect. The others will, to the practiced eye, reveal some flaw—though perhaps only so slight a defect as a grain that is not quite uniform. Among well-made pipes, those with minute flaws will smoke as satisfactorily as the most perfect specimens. A smoker who insists on having a perfect pipe should be prepared to spend as much as $100, an expense that seems needless considering the fact that excellent pipes can be obtained in the $5 to $25 range.

In general, the buyer is advised to select the pipe with the most eye appeal. It makes sense to examine the pipe for fissures, pits and mars, the most common defects, but rarely does the consumer encounter a pipe with faults that escaped detection at the factory. The rigid quality controls imposed on pipe making by modern manufacturers assure the consumer of a serviceable pipe.

Key to quality control is the shaping of a pipe. If a defect appears while the bowl, held in a vise, is being bored by a high speed bit, the pipe will either be scrapped or reshaped in such a way as to eliminate the fault. When the bowl has been bored, other defects may come to light while the remainder of the pipe is shaped on a frazing machine, a device that enables the machinist to follow the template in the manner of a locksmith copying a key. Again, if a defect comes to light, it is obviated by reshaping the pipe or, if necessary, discarding it altogether.

The transition of briar from a gnarled protuberance on a scraggly wind-bent tree to a beautifully grained pipe head is a process that may involve as many as one hundred operations. But the most important consideration remains the briar itself. Because the care and skill employed in choosing briar borders on finickiness, one may ask, "Will there always be enough briar available to manufacture good pipes?" For a century or so, it seems there will be an assured supply of briar. Should the supply ultimately fail—and the defection of cigarette smokers to the pipe suggests this may happen sooner than anticipated—it may be that briar substitutes will be employed, as they were during World War II when war raged across the briar-rich Mediterranean and shipping priorities bumped briar off cargo manifests.

Woods that have been and could be used in lieu of true briar include rhododendron and mountain laurel, burl-producing shrubs found in the mountains of our southeastern states and prized by tourist and home owner alike for their showy flowers and evergreen leaves. Another candidate is Texas mesquite, a kind of barberry whose roots often plunge as deep as 60 feet underground. Yew wood, called "fighting wood" by the Indians of the northeast, may also regain the popularity it enjoyed during the war.

But it appears that such fine briars as those from

Algeria will reign indefinitely as King so long as a single white heath tree flourishes, be it a native of the soil of Italy, France, Spain, Corsica, Sicily, Greece, or Asia Minor.

Long live—we hope—the briar!

CHAPTER 7

THE PIPE
FOR YOU

To the serious pipe smoker, buying a pipe may represent an adventure only slightly less terrifying and final than selecting a cemetery plot. However, a knowledge of certain fundamentals of pipe design can do much to divest the pipe shopper of his anxiety.

The following factors must be considered when buying a pipe:

1. Price
2. Function of the pipe
3. Choice of material
4. Shape of bowl
5. Shape of stem

Budgeting for pipe purchases is a purely personal matter, but with pipes, as with most wares on the market, the buyer will usually get pretty much what he pays for. The smoker is strongly advised, therefore, to spend as much money on a pipe as he can sensibly afford.

The matter of price decided, the buyer must ask

himself what sort of pipe he wishes. Does he desire a sporty pipe for outdoor smoking? A debonair and sophisticated pipe to display at the cocktail hour? A lightweight pipe that he can keep in his mouth for extended periods of time while he works with his hands? A comfortably heavy pipe to hold while reading or watching television? An exotic pipe that will, inevitably, direct conversation to the pipe smoker's favorite subject, pipe smoking? Whatever the purpose, the smoker should bear in mind that a pipe, like a hat, is an accessory; it should complement the smoker's physique and personality. Obviously, a corncob is a poor choice for a man who customarily wears a Homburg and sports a boutonniere, as is a dainty clay pipe for a brawny Turkish bath attendant.

More important than a man's activities, wardrobe, or waistline, however, in terms of com-pipe-ability, is physiognomy—the shape of one's face. Portly men with round faces look better with curved pipes than with the straight, long-stemmed pipes that favor slender faces. A mirror is perhaps the most reliable judge of which pipe flatters you. When picking out a pipe, hold it near your mouth and study the effect. If you feel it isn't pleasing, try other pipes until you find the one for you.

Often, of course, you will have to strike a compromise between looks and function. For reading, you may have to choose a rather long-stemmed pipe in the interest of preventing smoke from getting in your eyes. A curved stem, the easiest to hold with your teeth, may be required if you must work with the pipe in your mouth. Usually, however, it is possible to find a pipe that is both functional and flattering.

The ultimate decision of the style of pipe is an intimate one. But it will, in turn, provide—or at the very least suggest—an answer to the next question: What material will best suit the function of the pipe desired? For a lightweight pipe, a calabash may prove most suitable. Porcelain or meerschaum may oblige the most discerning connoisseur. Cherry-woods and corncobs appeal to the outdoor sportsman. But since briars are now available in such variety as to satisfy nearly every consideration, this discussion will confine itself to the briarwood pipe.

The size and shape of the pipe bowl are controlling considerations, for the depth of the bowl and the thickness of the walls determine, to some extent, whether the pipe will provide a cool smoke or a hot one. The larger the bowl, the greater the opportunity for dispersion of heat. The deeper the bowl, the cooler the smoke.

The shape of the bowl is important. Because the tobacco hole has a curved or rounded bottom, the bowl will tend to cake evenly, a factor that adds savor to the smoke while extending the life of the pipe.

These considerations weighed, the smoker is now confronted with the actual choice: which of the many shapes will he choose from among those that meet his specifications.

Consider the number of recognized pipe shapes available:

Billiard	Panel
Saddle pot bowl	Canadian
Large pot bowl	Slim billiard
Woodstock	Giant billiard
Apple	Four Square
Slim apple	Oom-Paul
Saddle apple	Prince
Slim saddle apple	Sickle
Saddle-bit Dublin	Bent
Large Dublin	Wellington
Author	Chubby
Oval bowl	Well
Bulldog	Woodstock
Light bulldog	Setter
Taper bulldog	Prince of Wales
Saddle bit bulldog	Topper
English saddle	Lumberman
Lovat	Bull Moose
Liverpool	Boer
Rhodesian	Scotch Pug
Egg	Pear

Actually, these can be grouped into six basic bowl shapes: the *pot* bowl, which has sides parallel and a larger chamber than other pipes; the *Dublin*, another pipe bowl formed by straight lines; bowls with curved lines are the *billiard* bowl, the *prince*, *pear* bowl, and *apple* bowl. The most popular bowls are, in order, the *billiard*, *apple*, and *pot*. Pipe styles are named not only for the bowl, but sometimes for the bit or the shank, a practice that was common with the old English clay pipes.

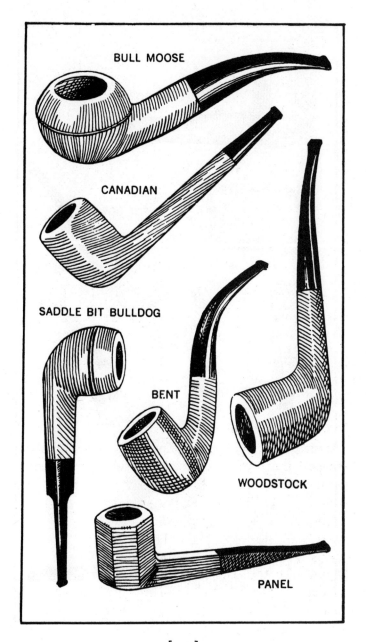

BULL MOOSE

CANADIAN

SADDLE BIT BULLDOG

BENT

WOODSTOCK

PANEL

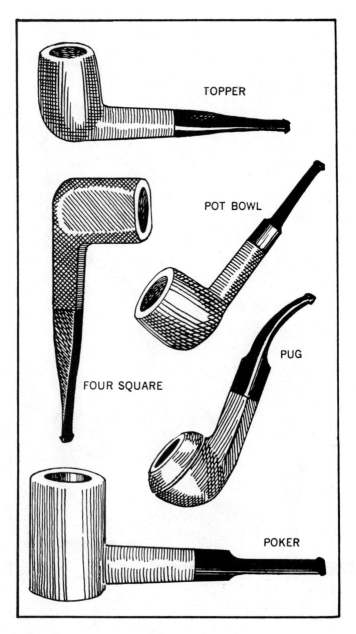

TOPPER

POT BOWL

FOUR SQUARE

PUG

POKER

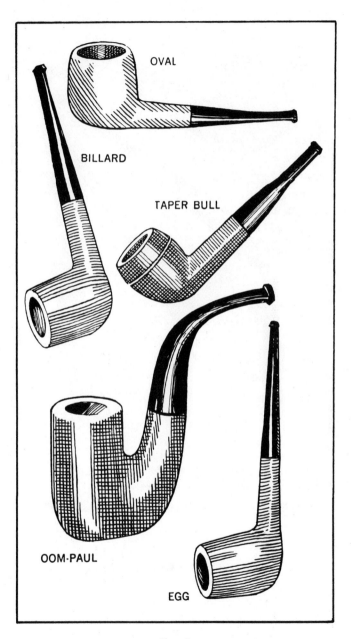

OVAL

BILLARD

TAPER BULL

OOM-PAUL

EGG

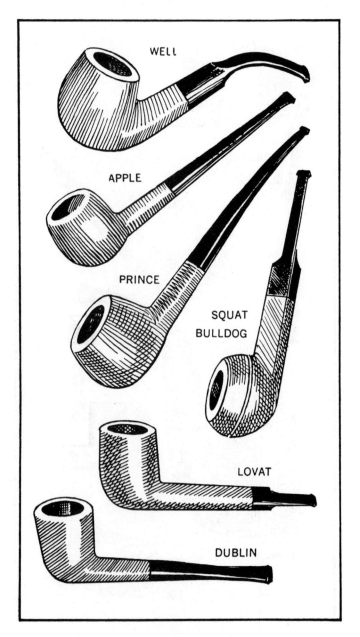

WELL

APPLE

PRINCE

SQUAT
BULLDOG

LOVAT

DUBLIN

The shank is the part of the pipe that unites bit (mouthpiece) and bowl. Basically, there are four styles of shank: *round*, *square*, *diamond*, and *oval*. The compatibility of the shank can contribute much or little to the over-all appearance of the pipe. Generally speaking, the longer the shank the shorter the stem (the upper section that terminates in the bit) and, conversely, the shorter the shank the longer the stem. Observance of this rule leads to pipes with pleasing proportions. In every case,

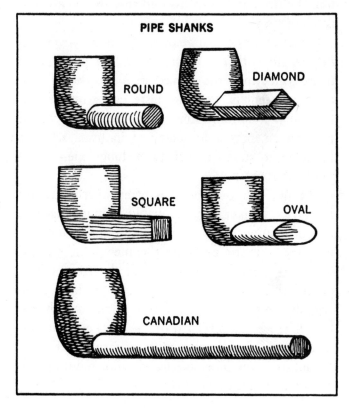

the shank and stem must achieve a perfect fit and a unity of line. Diamond-shaped shanks require diamond-shaped stems, just as oval shanks demand oval stems machined to match the shank.

Paramount in the design of the stem is the manner in which it couples to the shank. Push-fit stems are the best; with a slight push, executed with a twisting motion, the stem couples tightly to the shank. If perfectly designed, neither heat nor moisture will affect the fit. Assured of a good connection, the smoker can be assured that the pipe is not likely to break.

The thickness or gauge of the stem, however, has little to do with the efficiency of the pipe; arguments concerning the curved stem and the straight stem are needless. Personal taste can arbitrate this decision. While more difficult to clean, the curved stem has an inimitable poetry of its own, whereas the straight stem—especially a long one—has a rakish air about it.

The bit, or mouthpiece, is often overlooked by the novice smoker, who probably assumes that it is of as little importance as the hubcaps on an automobile. Yet it is, to continue the metaphor, as vital as a car's driver's seat. The seat determines how comfortable the driver will be, the bit how comfortable the pipe will feel. Shape of the mouth, nature of the teeth, strength of the jaws and gums— these are the factors that must govern selection of the bit, for if the pipe does not fit your mouth properly it is certain to grow sour.

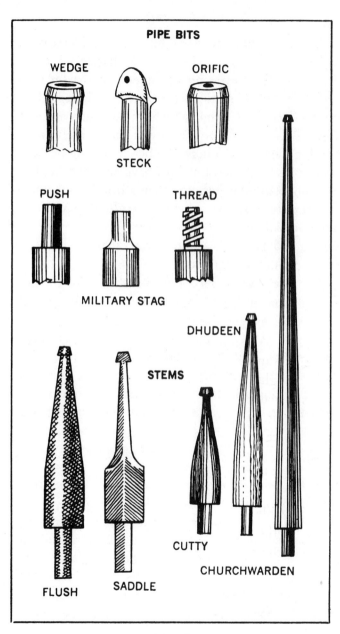

PIPE BITS

WEDGE   STECK   ORIFIC

PUSH   MILITARY STAG   THREAD

STEMS

DHUDEEN

FLUSH   SADDLE   CUTTY   CHURCHWARDEN

There are two kinds of bits, wide and narrow. Which to choose is, literally, a matter of taste. Three styles of opening at the end of the bit prevail: the wedge, steck, and orific. The latter offers only a small hole, from which smoke issues as from a jet. As a result, tongue bite is more likely with this bit than with others. Amber, ivory, bone, and other materials almost always have an orific lip, being too brittle to permit other kinds of openings.

The wedge is a very popular style. Its flat, wide opening admits a widely distributed stream of smoke and provides a good draft, making it easier to keep the pipe lighted.

The steck bit has its opening at the top of the lip. The smoke, therefore, avoids the tongue altogether, a boon to "wet" smokers.

Bits are generally made of vulcanite or pararubber, though special substances are sometimes employed to fashion dental bits that make minimal demands on false teeth. The best vulcanite stems are cut out of pressed sheets of rubber and turned on machines. Other stems are die-cut from round stock. Ebonite, bone, ivory, and amber are encountered on certain of the expensive pipes, despite the fact that some of these materials have a flavor that they impart to the tobacco. After long use, bone can produce a particularly disagreeable flavor.

Whether or not a stem should have a built-in filter is a controversy that has raged for years. Pro-filter folk argue that there is no reason why the pipe should not keep apace of our swiftly advancing technological civilization. Anyhow, they conclude, the darn thing tastes better with a filter. By lengthening the journey of the smoke and screening out impurities—tobacco particles, tars, and nicotine—filters, in theory if not in practice, cool and refine a smoke.

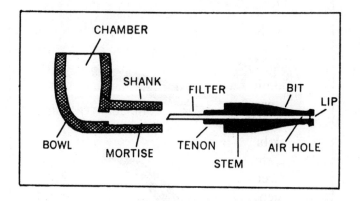

Those who are against anti-nicotine contraptions insist that filters tend to clog the stem of the pipe and produce an aftertaste. To keep a pipe smelling and smoking sweetly, it is enough, declare the contentious filterphobes, to clean a pipe thoroughly and regularly. But whether or not to use a filter will always remain a highly personal matter.

The stem is useful also as a means of determining the integrity of the manufacturer and dealer. Its quality, finish, and fit will reveal attention to detail or telltale carelessness.

Because stems are much more likely to break than bowls—at least in the case of briar pipes—the repair of stems deserves discussion. When, as sometimes happens, the smoker bites a hole through his fa-

STEM CURVES

ONE-EIGHTH CURVE

ONE-QUARTER CURVE

ONE-HALF CURVE

THREE-QUARTER CURVE

FULL CURVE

vorite vulcanite mouthpiece, the pipesmith can cut a new lip on the stem and burnish it so that it looks brand new, but it is cheaper and easier to have a new stem fitted by a pipe repair man.

When an expensive amber mouthpiece breaks close to the shank, the broken portion can be replaced with new amber. Indeed, many stems provide so many years of faithful service that they outlive their owners.

When the shape of the pipe has been selected, the purchaser must return to a consideration of the bowl, and then to a decision as to whether the overall workmanship is of satisfactory quality. Infatuation with mere "looks" has led many a pipe smoker to regret not having submitted the pipe to a thorough examination.

In briar, flame grain, straight grain, and bird's eye grain are the most rare grains, bird's eye grain being the least common of the three and therefore the most expensive. Most pipes combine two or more of these grains; it is the pipe that boasts entirely one kind of grain that is coveted by perfectionists. Quality of grain, however, does not affect the pipe's smoking performance, and nearly every grain, however common, is pleasing to the eye. More important, no two grains are exactly alike, and so every pipe—a $5 pipe with ordinary grain or a $75 pipe with perfect up-and-down straight grain—is unique.

The exterior surface of the pipe bowl may be smooth or rough. Pipes with the increasingly popular rough or pebbly surfaces are called "sandblast" models. They are easy to grip, have a rough and rugged air about them and, possibly, smoke a bit cooler than smooth finish pipes. Those who claim they smoke cooler argue that the rough finish affords greater surface for dispersion of heat but this seems to be tantamount to hairsplitting. Smooth pipes have always been and will continue to be admired. To buy a smooth finish or a sandblast is purely a personal matter.

Finishes of pipes vary greatly. Some are stained, others varnished—though the varnish is more truly a shellac. Some are merely oiled. Pipes with a completely natural finish (or matte finish) are among the most handsome. Pipes improve over the years as they exude, then re-absorb, oil particles, and matte finish pipes perform this function with the greatest ease.

The inside of the pipe bowl may consist of the natural briar or boast a lining of charcoal or meerschaum. Made from burned nut shells, the charcoal lining offers the buyer a pipe that may be said to have been pre-broken in. The cake provided by the manufacturer in the form of charcoal gives the novice smoker a head start in building up the desirable cake formed by smoking tobacco.

The meerschaum lining found in the better pipes also expedites the breaking in of a pipe, providing at the very outset a remarkably cool smoke. Every pipe smoker should have a couple of meerschaum-lined pipes to appreciate their special properties.

The do's and don'ts of buying a pipe are few and simple: do buy as expensive a pipe as you can afford, for pipes are no exception to the general rule that you get what you pay for. Do look for a pipe stamped "genuine" or "imported" briar. The terms are synonymous and assure you of an excellent pipe. Don't buy a pipe that does not bear a trade name or one whose trade name has been obliterated, for reputable manufacturers are proud of their products and advertise them. Finally, feel confident about buying a pipe. Centuries of experience, coupled with modern quality controls, have enabled the pipe maker to assure the pipe buyer that finding a good pipe is a briar-pipe cinch!

CHAPTER 8

THE TOBACCO FOR YOU

Save for flavoring agents, such as Xanthi, Latakia, Adrianople, and other Turkish tobaccos, as well as those imported from the Orient, virtually all of the pipe tobacco consumed by Americans is homegrown. This is much less true of cigarette and cigar tobaccos, for they sometimes contain a relatively high percentage of foreign leaf.

The tobaccos most often used in prepared American blends of pipe tobacco are white Burley, Virginia, and Maryland. White Burley comes from north-central Kentucky, southwestern West Virginia, Tennessee, southern Ohio, and southeastern Indiana. From Virginia—as well as from Florida, Georgia, and the Carolinas—comes Virginia tobacco, the best grade being Virginia Bright, a plant that stands nearly seven feet high and boasts pale green-gold leaves. Maryland tobacco is grown only in Maryland. A less familiar native tobacco is perique. Sweet and with a strong flavor, it is cultivated in Louisiana.

Tobacco is a broad-leaved perennial plant that flourishes in a great variety of soils; it may be grown successfully in latitudes ranging from southern Canada to the tropics and in areas where even wheat and corn cannot thrive. Flavor and quality of tobacco leaf, however, are profoundly influenced by local soil and climate conditions. Tobacco culture, therefore, focuses on making the best possible use of specialized conditions; a heavy clay soil that encourages the growth of one kind of tobacco may be useless for another kind requiring light, sandy soil. The methods of cultivating the various strains of tobacco, however, are essentially the same.

Seed—a heaping teaspoonful will provide plants enough to cover an acre of field—is generally sown in January, February, or March after the ground has been harrowed, plowed, and fertilized. Often the seed is mixed with fertilizer. Once a manual operation, sowing is now accomplished by machine, as is the transplanting that takes place when the young seedlings spring up. The young plants are spaced at precise intervals—in Kentucky about 3½ feet apart in the row, about 2½ feet apart in Virginia.

As soon as 10 to 15 leaves have appeared on the plant, a few of the bottom leaves are picked and discarded as are, often, the blossoms and uppermost parts of the plants. Called "topping," this practice encourages maximum growth of the plant's most desirable leaves, increasing their size, body, and flavor-producing nicotine content.

Some 30 or 40 days later, usually in August or September, the plants are ready for harvesting. In the case of fire-cured tobaccos, like those of Kentucky and Tennessee, the plants are cut within inches of their base and remain on the ground until they have wilted sufficiently to permit handling without damaging the leaves. The yellow tobacco called flue-cured is harvested in a different manner. The leaves are picked as they ripen and carried to the curing barn in small bunches tied to sticks. Often the field must be gone over as many as six times to obtain leaves at the proper stage of ripeness.

The harvesting done, the leaves are cured, or dried. Here it must be emphasized that for every tobacco there is a distinctive, particular curing process, for the curing plays a vital role in determining the tobacco's flavor and aroma. Which method of curing to use is determined by the regional characteristics of the tobacco. Some crops are dried with smoke. Others are air-cured. In flue-curing, the leaves are exposed to radiant heat conducted by flues, or pipes, operated by a furnace.

After the cured tobacco has been graded, most varieties are bunched and stacked in piles and offered for sale at auction. Some tobaccos are first fermented and aged; perique, for example, whose properties will be discussed later, is fermented under pressure for a period of 12 months.

Through improved methods of cultivation and the development of efficient machinery, tobacco culture has become a highly specialized and exact science. But the proliferating technology and know-how of our time is less than foolproof. Droughts and frosts, such parasites as beetles and moths, and diseases caused by fungi, bacteria, and viruses can destroy a crop overnight.

Fortunately, the pipe smoker need not be concerned with the risks that attend tobacco culture.

His sole concern is to find the tobacco, or more likely the combination of tobaccos, that best suits his taste. An easy matter? Scarcely, for there are more name brands of pipe tobacco than there are of cigarettes. Short of giving each brand a fair trial, there is no way of determining which prepared blend—if any—will suit his taste.

Trial-and-error selection is made somewhat easier by the fact that many leading tobacco manufacturers and distributors sell sample assortments of their blends, enabling the smoker to purchase at a reasonable price five or six brands at once, each in an appealingly diminutive package. When such "kits" are not available, smokers sometimes find it possible to try new blends by trading tobacco with other pipesters who are chasing that will-o'-the-wisp, the perfect smoke.

Mixing and blending your own tobaccos, however, is an art that provides rich rewards in terms of education, esthetics, and economy. In his Epicurean experiments, the pipester can learn to make the best use of the best qualities of each type of tobacco.

Of all the tobaccos, Burley is probably the most popular. There are two kinds: Kentucky Burley and white Burley. Clean and cool-smoking, both may be smoked straight. Because of its rather bland flavor and aroma, white Burley is ideal for diluting the strength of such strong tobaccos as latakia, perique, and Turkish varieties. Slightly stronger, but nonetheless mild, is Kentucky Burley, which can also be smoked straight. Whatever the blend you may be using, it can be "cut" with either Burley, as evidenced by the fact that many name brands on the market contain as much as 80 percent Burley. Small wonder that Burley is the second largest tobacco crop in this country.

Farther south, Virginia tobacco—the most desirable grade of which is Virginia Bright—is king. Smoked straight, it will bite, which makes all the more amazing this account of a smoking contest published in an 18th-century "smoker's companion":

> In a public room at Langdon Hills, in Essex, the conversation chancing to turn on smoking, a farmer of the name of Williams, boasting of the great quantity of tobacco he could consume at a sitting, challenged the room to produce his equal. Mr. Bowtell, the proprietor of the great bootshop (in) Skinner Street, and remarkable for smoking pipes beyond computation, traveling his round at that time, chanced to be present and immediately agreed to enter the lists with him for five pounds a-side. A canister of [Virginia] tobacco was placed by the side of each man at eight o'clock in the evening, when they began the match. Smoking very fast, by the time the clock had struck twelve, they had each finished sixteen pipes when the farmer, through the dense atmosphere, was observed to turn pale. He still continued, however, dauntlessly on, but, at the end of the eighteenth pipe, fell stupefied off his

chair. The victory was adjudged to his opponent who, calling for an extra glass of grog, actually finished his twentieth pipe before he retired for the night.

Though modern smokers are advised to eschew such heroics, they should experiment fully with the many varieties of Virginia tobacco.

Virginia Bright is one of the best of the Virginia tobaccos. It is cured by flues that conduct an even, moisture-regulated and smoke-free heat through the curing barns.

A slow-burning tobacco with a cooler and sweeter taste is Virginia Bright Leaf. It is one of the oldest varieties of flue-cured tobacco. Both the curing process and the cutting impart a pleasing taste to Virginia Bright Leaf.

Somewhat of a misnomer is the name Virginia Sun-Cured—the common name for a type of air-cured tobacco. In truth, nearly all of today's so-called sun-cured tobaccos are barn-cured. This rich tobacco is now generally cured in the same manner as burley.

Virginia is also the home of the world-renowned Cavendish tobaccos. Flavored with honey, rum, maple sugar, molasses, or similar substances, Cavendish is a rich, dark, sweet tobacco that can be used as a base or as a flavoring agent. Reputedly named after Lord William Cavendish, Duke of Newcastle, Cavendish comes in many varieties: shredded Cavendish, Cavendish dark plug cut, Honey Cavendish, and Virginia Cavendish. It is surely the experimenter's delight, for it blends readily with both Burley and Virginia tobaccos. Highly smokeable in its own right, Cavendish may comprise as much as 90 percent of a mixture. It is most effective when combined with Burley and flavored with perique, latakia, or one of the many Turkish tobaccos.

Cavendish may also refer to Virginia and Maryland tobaccos that have undergone processing similar to the true Cavendish. Strictly speaking, however, Maryland tobacco is a distinctive flavoring agent and has little in common with Cavendish-type Maryland tobaccos. True Maryland tobacco is, not surprisingly, indigenous to Maryland, thriving on the sandy soil in the southern part of The Old Line State. It burns slowly. It blends unobtrusively. It is, therefore, ideal for correcting a hotly burning blend, or one that is too flavorful.

The most adventuresome opportunities for flavoring are afforded by certain tobaccos raised abroad. As the flavor and bouquet of grapes may vary from vineyard to vineyard, even in the same province or upon the same hillside, so, too, do tobaccos vary greatly, influenced by such factors as rainfall, temperature, sunshine, altitude, and soil properties. Turkish tobaccos, for example, owe their excellence to an environment that is ideal for tobacco cultivation, even though one early writer contended that the Turk's penchant for cultivating and consuming tobacco can be attributed to his philosophical temperament. He states, "Without being lazy, the Turk does not like to hurry. 'Haste comes from the devil and patience from God,' he says." That nearly all of the tobaccos from the Near East are called Turkish is a recognition of the fact that the Turks once held sway over nearly all of the neighboring countries.

Early writings have this to say about Turkish tobacco: "At Constantinople the dealers sell smoking tobacco cut very fine in long, silky bunches of blond color. *Iavach* is the name for the mild quality; *orta* designates the average strength; *tokan aklen* the sharp tasting, and *sert* the very strong." Today, the best known Turkish tobaccos are Djebel, Adrianople, Xanthi, Macedonian, Smyrna Samsoun, and Trebizond.

Djebel and Xanthi are held by many experts to be among the very finest of tobaccos. Xanthi, in fact, is sometimes called the Queen of Tobaccos. Sweet, full-bodied, and highly aromatic, it is used sparingly in blends; this is fortunate, for the quantity of Xanthi available at any given time is limited. A first cousin to Xanthi is Djebel, a more light-bodied and lightly flavored tobacco. Both tobaccos burn well.

Adrianople is popular with Asians and Europeans for its neutral taste and full-bodied aroma, but very little of the tobacco is imported into the United States.

Macedonian tobaccos, native to that region of Greece, have considerable appeal. Their aroma is soporific. Their taste is lightly sweet. They burn well and can be used either as a flavoring agent or as a base.

Smyrna burns slowly but dominates flavor quickly. It should, therefore, be used with great moderation, as should any strongly flavored tobacco.

Samsoun is often regarded as a panacea for all the ills attending any blend. Its taste is distinctive and delightful. It adds zest to the most lackluster of blends and boasts ideal burning qualities. No blending table should lack Samsoun.

One of the strongest flavors is imparted by Trebizond. Though it is grown near the district of Samsoun, its flavor is considerably more robust than that of the neighboring tobacco.

The virtues of Turkish tobacco considered, how much of this vigorous agent should be used by the do-it-yourself tobacco blender? Although taste and experience will prove the ultimate guide, the novice is not likely to err too grievously if he begins by adding one part of Turkish tobacco to 15 parts of Burley and/or Virginia.

Even greater caution must be exercised when latakia or perique is used. Latakia owes its heavy, musky flavor to a unique curing process: the plant, including the flowers, is hung over a fire composed of aromatic herbs. While the leaves of most tobacco plants are the most useful material, in the case of latakia it is the stems and ribs that are used. Nearly black, often distinctively oily and broodingly sweet, a little latakia goes a long way. As small a quantity as one ounce will impart its commanding flavor to one pound of tobacco. It very nearly requires a bona fide Syrian to stand up to a mixture containing more than, say, 10 to 20 percent latakia.

Perique has the most distinctive flavor of any tobacco, which is to say that only perique tastes like perique. Legend has it that one Pierre Chenet stole the process for making this spicy tobacco from American Indians who had found a way to ferment tobacco leaves in their own juice. There is, apparently, more to perique than its unique processing. Baffling to botanists is the fact that while perique seeds have been planted all over the world, they will not, cannot, do not choose to grow anywhere save on a wedge-shaped tract of land to the west of New Orleans. Perique has a heady tang, burns slowly, and excels as an agent for counteracting the bite of hot-burning tobaccos.

In considering the burning qualities of a tobacco, one must also be mindful of the "cut" of tobacco. When a leaf is cut into long, string-like strips, the tobacco is said to be ribbon cut. It will stay lighted for the shreds encourage the circulation of air. If the leaf is cut into small squares, which tend to burn slowly, the tobacco is called chop cut. No matter how a single leaf is cut, it may be called a long cut to distinguish it from leaves that are cut after being pressed together to form a cake. Any kind of cut from a cake is called plug cut.

To blend tobaccos successfully, one must shrewdly assay combustion, texture, flavor, and aroma factors, which doubtless explains why this aspect of tobaccology is considered an exacting and exquisite art.

CHAPTER 9

HOW TO ENJOY SMOKING A PIPE

Obtaining pleasure from a pipe is an easy matter. Remember this, no matter what you may read in this chapter or elsewhere. Discussed in minute detail, the simplest activity or act may assume awesome, forbidding proportions. Upon reading a thoroughly conscientious, step-by-step description of the technique for tying one's shoe, almost any reader would elect to go barefooted. Thus it is with dissertations on how to smoke a pipe.

Anyone can learn to smoke a pipe with ease and pleasure. To be sure, there are a few do's and don'ts to keep in mind, a few elementary facts to be learned if you are to obtain maximum enjoyment from your pipe.

In light of this, one may ask: Why it is that more smokers who try a pipe do not stick with it? According to one American pipe expert, the answer is that the approach of the average man to smoking is all too casual, as if the very fact of his masculinity conferred upon him a special knowledge of the art. This man will study, with great humility and diligence, the arts and secrets of hunting, fishing, golf and carpentry, but he will not spend a few minutes learning the fundamentals of pipe smoking.

Pipe smoking is easy—admittedly not quite as

easy as lighting a match and putting it to the bowl, but as easy as, say, tying one's shoe.

First, a smoker, unless he is a magician, requires three materials in order to smoke a pipe: a pipe, tobacco, and a flame. In days gone by a gentleman carried with him at all times a complete smoking kit, consisting of a tobacco box, a pair of tongs with which to seize a burning coal and light his pipe, and a tobacco stopper—a device for pushing the burning leaves down into his pipe. Today, if the smoker's true desire is not to attract attention but merely to smoke his pipe, he may go encumbered only by pipe, pouch, and paper matches.

Having bought his pipe, the new smoker must learn how to properly break it in. On this delicate matter, the advice offered in the 1800's by John Baine remains, for the most part, virtually unchallenged:

> Begin by handling a new pipe very gingerly. A new pipe is like a new baby and must be treated tenderly. Some smokers carefully wet the inside of the bowl (unless it is lined with charcoal or meerschaum) before putting the tobacco in a new pipe. This we believe to be the proper thing as it removes any new or sticky taste that may have been left in the pipe.
>
> Your new pipe is now ready for use. Some smokers, before inserting the tobacco, put in a piece of blotting paper in the bottom of the

bowl. DO NOT do this! It is said that blotting paper absorbs the flavor of the tobacco.

Put in your tobacco but don't fill it to the top of the bowl. Be careful, in lighting your tobacco, not to burn the rim of the bowl. Smoke very leisurely at first, gently breaking in your pipe until every part of it seems to be hardened to the heat. Keep this up for five or six smokes. Then you and your pipe can "rough it" anywhere on earth.

In filling your pipe be careful not to pack it in too tight, so that the bowl becomes choked up and the tobacco refuses to burn. Put your tobacco in fairly loose, and after a few puffs push it gently down in the bowl and keep doing this at intervals until your smoke is finished. This prevents the pipe from going out and creates moisture enough so that there is no danger of it biting the tongue.

After you have finished smoking, remove the ashes by spooning them out with a little instrument (Author's Note: a smoker's companion) that is made for that purpose and which can be bought for about twenty-five cents. If any refuse remains in the bowl after it has been smoked, it can be removed by knocking the bowl in the hand.

The original coating should never be disturbed, for it is really the fine flavor—the divine aroma—which clings to a pipe and is to every true smoker a delight.

Here Baine states—and we must disagree with him—that the smoker should be "the possessor of at least three good briar pipes [and that] this being the case none of these pipes should be smoked oftener than once in three days." Twirl in his grave though he may, Baine deserves to be rebuked for vouchsafing such nonsense. The modern pipe smoker, because of the greater pleasure modern pipes afford, is quite likely to smoke several pipefuls of tobacco a day. If he were to abide by Baine's advice and smoke each of his pipes only once every three days, our modern smoker would be compelled to carry with him six, eight, or ten pipes to get through the day, an impractical and patently absurd notion.

More sensibly, the modern pipe smoker will smoke one pipe several times during the day, then give it a well-deserved rest. For this reason, the pipe smoker is well advised to have at least seven pipes, one for each day, enabling each pipe to enjoy a week's vacation, preferably upright in a pipe rack where it can enjoy a thorough and leisurely airing.

Baine did know what he was talking about when he suggested that the smoker take it slow and easy when breaking in a pipe. The French writer Herment, for example, suggests that a new pipe be filled only a quarter of the way the first five or six times it is smoked; only half full the next ten smokings; and a few times at the three-quarter level before commencing normal smoking procedure. This makes good sense, but it is a bit more complicated than the advice offered by pipesmiths at the Carl

Weber factory. They say it is enough to fill the pipe one-fifth full the first time it is smoked, two-fifths full the second time, three-fifths on the third day, then four-fifths, and, on the fifth day, full to the top—a simple rule of five that will assure you of breaking in your new pipe properly. Each pipeful should be smoked all the way down.

Other modern experts counsel with this adage: "Fill your pipe first with a child's hand, then a woman's hand, and, finally, a man's."

Once the bowl is full, the smoker should lightly apply pressure to the top of the bowl with his forefinger. This has the effect of evening the surface of the tobacco. An even, uniform surface is essential if the pipe is to be evenly lit. If the tobacco has been packed properly, it will have a slight springiness. Having smoothed and lightly compressed the surface of the tobacco, one should draw on the pipe stem. Often, after lighting the pipe, it is a good idea to again lightly tamp down the tobacco; this lessens the possibility of the pipe going out.

Does the pipe draw hard? If so, there may be a shred of tobacco clogging the air hole that leads into the pipe stem. This means that the bowl must be emptied and repacked. Sometimes the blockage may be in the pipe stem itself. It may be possible to remove the obstruction with a pipe cleaner. Generally speaking, a tight pipe is not a right pipe, and must be repacked.

When air flows through the pipe too freely, the situation can often be remedied by adding some thumb pressure to the top of the bowl, and another pinch of tobacco. At any rate, a loose pipe is preferable to a tight one.

Unfortunately, a pipe may be packed too loosely *and* too tightly. The center tobacco may be looser than one side or the other, or packed more tightly than the tobacco near the wall of the bowl. This happens only when the pipe has been filled in a haphazard manner, but the results, over a period of time, can ruin a pipe by causing the bowl to heat unevenly and crack or scorch.

If the inexperienced smoker has a little difficulty at first in properly filling the pipe, he must be patient. Too, he may find it easier to fill his pipe with a coarse cut tobacco than with a fine one.

Here, then, are some do's and don'ts on the subject of filling a pipe:

DO fill the pipe a pinch at a time, starting with a small pinch to cover the bottom of the bowl.

DO tamp the tobacco evenly.

DO even the lighting surface with forefinger pressure.

DON'T imitate those dunderheads who fill a pipe by plunging it into a jar or pouch and ramming it full with a forefinger.

DON'T try to smoke your pipe if it draws tightly; repack it!

DON'T forget that a pipe cannot be filled correctly unless the ashes and tobacco from the last smoke have been removed from the bowl.

Now to the matter of seasoning a pipe. The subject can be dismissed quickly; the modern pipe seldom requires seasoning. For one thing, many of today's briars boast meerschaum linings. They are, in a sense, self-seasoning, assuming that you break in your pipe properly. And, praise be, there are now a host of pre-caked pipes on the market, pipes whose bowls have been factory-lined with a thin caking made from the charcoal of burned nut shells. This charcoal lining makes it a quite simple matter for the owner of a new pipe to build up the cake that will improve both pipe and tobacco flavor. In view of the attributes of the modern briar, heed not the persuasive arguments some smokers martial for seasoning a pipe with alcohol, honey, brandy or cognac. Such recipes, with their attendant rituals, are more likely to harm than help a pipe achieve maturity.

On the subject of lighting a pipe, Baine is very much to the point: "Be careful in lighting your tobacco not to burn the rim of the bowl." This advice applies whether the smoker employs a match or lighter for lighting up. Which to employ is entirely a matter of personal preference. Some pipe smokers favor the lighters designed for pipes, many of which are both dependable and ingenious, enabling the smoker to direct a steady flame into the pipe bowl. Others, especially of the older generation of pipesters, contend, on philosophical grounds, that a fine briar, with its rich patina, is not compatible with such "a newfangled gadget" as a lighter.

If you do use a match, let its head burn off so that you don't ruin your smoke with phosphorous and sulphur fumes. Whether you use a match or a lighter, light the pipe as evenly as possible by holding the bowl upright—never tilt it, a practice as senseless as holding an umbrella upside down or sideways—drawing strongly and circling the lighted match around the bowl. In this way, you will assure an even light and, assuming the bowl has been properly packed, a pipe that will draw easily.

On rare occasions, such as camping, hunting or fishing expeditions, or a stint of National Guard or Scoutmaster duty, you may find an opportunity to light your pipe by placing in its bowl a glowing ember removed from a campfire. More often an indoor fireplace will provide this opportunity. No matter the circumstances, choose an ember big enough to do the job but small enough so that it will not burn the rim of the bowl. A light obtained from an ember is surely the most romantic means of lighting a pipe.

Some do's and don'ts on the subject of lighting a pipe:

DO light the pipe evenly.

DO consider the usefulness of the lowly match.

DON'T apply match to bowl until the match fumes have burned away.

DO hold the bowl upright when lighting the pipe.

DO make sure, before lighting, that the pipe stem is clear, by blowing through the mouthpiece.

From the very first pipeful of tobacco, one must be careful to empty and clean the pipe properly. The spoon, alluded to by Baine, offers the safest way of removing the ashes without damaging the cake forming in the bowl. Lacking a spoon, the round end of a nail file may be used. No matter what implement is used, the task must be performed gently. Emptying the bowl by striking it against a hard object should always be avoided. If a pipe smoker's ashtray, with its cork knob, is not available, the palm of the hand can be struck with the bowl to dislodge ash. Few novices realize that the risk of breakage extends to the pipe stem as well as the cake. It is also possible, though not probable, that the briar shank itself, its knots composed of congeries of tiny fibers, will crack, given a sharp blow under certain circumstances.

Cleaning a pipe can be an agreeable or annoying task, depending on one's temperament. When removed from the classification of an elaborate ritual, it is a pleasant diversion and not without tangible rewards. One writer of old speaks of the conscientious connoisseur whose pipes "gleam and glitter in the firelight like newly-shelled chestnuts." Such a picture is incentive enough to keep one's briars looking their best.

One unbreakable rule among true pipe devotees is that every pipe should be cleaned regularly. Pipe cleaners—highly pliable wires girded with absorbent material—make this task an easy one. The smoker has only to run the pipe cleaner through the stem a few times and remove the ash from the bowl. Then air should be encouraged to circulate through the bowl by hanging or standing the pipe up to dry. One need not go as far as M. Reboux of the Academy of Sciences of Paris, who urged, "Clean your pipe frequently, if not five times a day—should you be a heavy smoker," but smokers should not delay cleaning a pipe when it is necessary.

Every few months the pipe should be cleaned thoroughly. This entails removing the stem, cleaning it with a single and then a doubled-up pipe cleaner, and swabbing the filter, if there is one, and shank boring with pipe cleaner fluid, though alcohol (it can be flavored with oil of clove or oil of wintergreen) is highly satisfactory. Chamois leather can be used to buff the pipe to a pleasing luster. Rubbing the pipe along the side of one's nose is another way to polish the pipe, for the briar has a natural affinity for the oil in your skin.

From time to time the smoker must also check the thickness of the cake in the bowl. If its thickness exceeds ⅛ of an inch, the bowl should be reamed as evenly as possible. A reamer, a small, metal object obtainable at any pipe store, simplifies the chore. Adjusted to the desired size (you can sometimes buy a reamer of the exact size you require), the reamer blade is inserted in the bowl and gently rotated to pare down the cake. Used with too much enthusiasm, the blade may bore all the way through the cake, either at the bottom or sides of the bowl. Loss of the cake anywhere in the bowl may lead to a burn-through.

Why is cake so important in pipe smoking? Cake is the material that protects the briar from the excessive heat of burning tobacco. Cake is, then, a fire wall. When the cake becomes too thick, however, the bowl may crack because of the disparity between the temperature of the cake and that of the bowl. Furthermore, if permitted to thicken indefinitely, the cake will succeed in reducing drastically the size of the bowl.

Some experts insist that only the outer part of the cake should be scraped out. Others declare that layers of char mean nothing; the cake must be constantly maintained at a thickness of a penny. A few heretics favor scraping all of the cake off and starting anew each time, but arguments for this scorched bowl policy strike this writer as being foolish and feeble.

A pipe that has been properly broken in, properly cleaned, and properly filled and lighted cannot fail to yield pleasure.

CHAPTER 10

PIPE
ACCESSORIES

GREAT CARE should be exercised in the selection of pipe accessories, for, along with the pipe, tobacco, and technique of smoking, they will determine how much or how little you will enjoy smoking your pipe.

Pipe cleaners are indispensable and, fortunately, inexpensive. Some have a soft, fluffy quality; others are bristle-like. The coarse or stiff pipe cleaners are useful for removing deposits of gum, while the softer ones are ideal for absorbing oily and liquid matter that has accumulated in the pipe. In recent years, the tapered pipe cleaner—narrow at one end and nearly twice as wide at the other—has won favor. Because the modern pipe cleaner is available in a wide variety of sizes and textures, there is virtually no excuse for poor pipe maintenance.

For the proper cleaning of a pipe, the smoker is advised to make frequent use of the pipe-cleaner fluids now available on the market. They have solvent qualities that dissolve accretions of gum and tar in the pipe, while imparting a fresh aroma to the bowl, stem, and mouthpiece. Such fluids are also known as pipe sweeteners.

The usual method of sweetening a pipe is to wipe out the inside of the bowl with a few drops of the liquid on a bit of cloth or cotton. (Some experienced smokers have been known to mix a few drops of rum or brandy into a pipeful of tobacco, the ensuing smoke acting as a sweetener.)

Too few modern pipe smokers have a proper appreciation of the humidor—or tobacco jar, as it is called on the continent. As suggested by its name, the humidor prevents tobacco from drying out. But the greater joy of the humidor is that it conserves and improves tobacco, enabling the smoker to blend old tobacco with new and thereby transfer the flavor of one filling to the other. Whether the humidor is made of metal, plastic, wood, ivory, horn, stone, or clay, it should be airtight—not only to keep moisture in, but also to keep unwelcome odors out. For this purpose, most humidors have a gasket fitted either to the mouth of the jar or to its lid.

The better humidors also contain a humidifying agent. It may be a piece of porous clay, soapstone, or plastic material, which replaces the moisture that evaporates within the jar. Some smokers provide their own humidifying agent, using a piece of apple, orange, or lemon peel, or a few drops of rum.

The main function of the humidor is to keep the tobacco in prime smoking condition, to maintain the state of the tobacco, as nearly as possible, as it was at the time of purchase.

Furthermore, the humidor is a pleasant adjunct to the ritual of lighting up. When the prospect of a smoke beckons, the smoker can look forward to opening the jar and inhaling the heady promise of the aroma that a pipe and match will soon bring to life. A minor factor is the slight advantage in economy offered by the humidor. Able to store tobacco for long periods, the smoker can buy it in large quantities and realize a slight saving.

It may be said that the tobacco pouch is, in a sense, a portable humidor, being an airtight container for the storage of tobacco. It suffers, of course, the disadvantages of being smaller and much less durable than its counterpart. The three most popular pouches are the zipper pouch, the circular rubber pouch, and the folding roll-up pouch. Pouches made of or lined with plastic or latex rubber are very desirable. Whether the pouch is made of leather, rubber, cellophane, silk, or pig's bladder, it should fulfill these functions:

1. It should keep the tobacco fresh, moist, and fragrant for a long time.
2. It should be big enough so that the smoker can fill his pipe with as little spillage as possible.
3. It should not impart any flavor of its own to the tobacco.
4. It should be pliable, so that the tobacco it contains does not break or crumble.
5. It should be of a size that fits easily into your pocket.

Considering these functions, it appears that the roll-up pouch is, in general, best suited to the smoker's needs, for it is airtight, unfolds to a generous size, and satisfies the other requirements for a good pouch.

If it is true, as some philosophers maintain, that a particular moment may call for a particular pipe, then a pipe rack is indispensable, for it permits the smoker to examine at a glance his array of pipes. Pipes strewn about in a desk drawer or box do not lend themselves to ready inspection. Here it should be pointed out that certain pipes, such as fragile clays and meerschaums, may require individual boxes. But the rugged, handsome briar is amenable to being displayed.

There are few more satisfying sights than a row of pipes ranged in a rack, but a pipe rack also serves a utilitarian purpose by insisting that the pipe stand upright.

Should the head be up or down? Georges Herment, a knowledgeable and entertaining writer on the subject of the pipe, states flatly, "One can, indeed, buy so-called 'pipe holders' in which the mouthpiece is held uppermost. We pass these by without comment, leaving such stupidity to expose itself." But the *Weber Guide to Pipes and Pipe Smoking* refutes Herment with this excellent argument: "The vertical position of the pipe allows moisture in the stem and shank to run down into the bowl, where it will evaporate or be consumed in the next smoke."

The question of ashtrays is less troublesome; almost any sizeable ashtray will suffice. But the best are those fitted with a rubber, leather, or cork knocker, against which the bowl of the pipe may be rapped with no risk of injury.

PIPE ACCESSORIES

PIPESTAND

HUMIDOR

PIPE CLEANERS

SMOKERS' COMPANION

PIPE REAMER

TOBACCO POUCH

TOBACCO POUCH

One of the handiest accessories available to the pipe smoker is the "smoker's companion"—a metal utensil fitted with a spoon, pick, and tamper. For packing tobacco down into the pipe while smoking, the tamper is more efficient—and more pleasing to the eyes of others—than, say, a pencil. The pick is useful for unclogging the air passage, while the spoon makes it easy to scoop out ashes in the bowl without damaging the cake at the bottom.

Reamers are also useful gadgets. Boasting adjustable cutting edges, they make it possible to enlarge the bowl of an overcaked pipe. In addition, they are designed to pare away the cake evenly so that one is not likely to crack or gouge the cake or bowl.

Other accessories include windcaps for outdoor smoking that keep tobacco from blowing away or burning out, atomizers for moistening tobacco, and buttons and caps that protect burning tobacco from juices in the heel of the pipe.

Although not absolutely essential to pipe smoking, these accessories will greatly extend the life of your pipe and amplify the pleasures of smoking.

Best Tobacco

CHAPTER 11

PIPE ETIQUETTE

Too often, the word *tact* is used to designate what is mere diplomacy. In simple truth, tact means the practice of thoughtfulness in all relationships. All good manners derive from basic kindness and so there are, or should be, a few rules for social smoking—rules that no gentlemen, or even men, will choose to flout.

The following rules are so obvious that the reader will hardly need to be reminded of them. But the new smoker will do well to bear them in mind:

1. Never smoke where there is a sign warning you it is prohibited in that place.
2. Don't smoke in any public place where you can sense or see it is annoying anybody.
3. Don't smoke in an elevator.
4. Don't smoke while you are part of a dense crowd.
5. Always ask permission to smoke when you are a guest.
6. Always ask permission of a lady who is *your* guest.
7. Never empty the burned-out tobacco (dottle) into a tiny ashtray. Never spill it anywhere.
8. Don't tap your pipe or knock it against

some other object, nervously wave it when you talk, or use it in any way that may distract from somebody else's talk. Remember that the pipe is a symbol of harmony, pleasure, amity, and even peace—so handle and use it gracefully.

9. Do be alert to the one real danger of pipe smoking—the possibility of burning ashes setting something afire. The pipe is the least dangerous of smokes, since the burning tobacco is contained within the bowl, but nevertheless the smoker should exercise care at all times.

As an example of what you must *not* do with your pipe, take the case of one American who was summarily ejected from the Casino in Monte Carlo after he had puffed up a smoke screen so dense that the croupier used his handkerchief to wipe his streaming eyes!

This brings us to the rather painful fact (painful to all gentlemanly pipe smokers) that there are persons, as well as other lesser animals, who are allergic to tobacco smoke. To inflict discomfort on others, however innocently, while enjoying the peculiar and calming pleasure of a beloved pipe presents a delicate social problem, for there are men and women so courteous and unselfish they would rather suffer than ask the smoker to give up his pipe. The late George Kauffman, a famous playwright and director, was such a man. It took Mr. Kauffman nine years before he could bring himself to ask his producer friend, Sam Harris, to refrain from smoking while they were together in the producer's office.

There are ways, if a man is sensitive to the feelings of others, to detect the first signs of discomfort and/or allergy. If a lady uses her handkerchief to shield her nose or dab at her eyes or if somebody coughs there is only one thing to do—apologize and put away your pipe.

The true facts in a dramatic case involving the famous English star, the late Robert Lorraine, and a harlequin Great Dane constitute a unique story in the annals of pipe smoking. Mr. Lorraine and the Great Dane opened at the Little Theater in a play called *The Master of the Inn*.

Mr. Lorraine was nearly as famous for his good manners as for his acting and so the out-of-town tryouts all went smoothly. But on opening night in New York Mr. Lorraine decided that the use of his pipe would give added flavor to his role. That night the star made his entrance with the dog leashed to one hand and his pipe in the other. Unfortunately, the ventilation blew smoke in the dog's direction. Opening-night nerves may explain Mr. Lorraine's lax hold on the leash. Befogged by smoke, the huge canine let out a howl and bounded toward the footlights, cleared them and the orchestra pit in one beautiful leap, and fled up the aisle.

The startled cries of lady first-nighters compounded the catastrophic confusion onstage and throughout the audience. An usher standing in the rear hastily opened a door that led to the lobby and the Great Dane made his great exit! A drama reviewer wrote, "A handsome Great Dane that was introduced into the first act promptly leaped over the footlights and left the theater before one of the critics could bite him." The poor dog was never allowed to perform again; a Russian wolfhound stepped into the role and was subsequently signed up and delivered to Hollywood and stardom. The kindly Robert Lorraine, a favorite of George Bernard Shaw, later apologized to the Great Dane and sent him a chocolate pipe when he sired four handsome pups!

On the positive side of the smoking picture, many women have attested to the appeal of the aroma of a rich pipe burning its fine tobacco. There is, they insist, an almost irresistible quality in the masculine bouquet of soap, tobacco, and (perhaps) Bay Rum, and this is especially so when the pipe is a carefully chosen adjunct to the well-groomed man who is smoking. There is a nicety in the choice and selection of a particular pipe to enhance the man's clothes; for example, a beautiful meerschaum sets off, or is set off by, a tweed tailored on Saville Row or Bond Street—or so many worldly ladies aver.

The robust cherrywood pipe complements Bermuda shorts. To the gentleman in a dinner jacket, the calabash contributes its own *elan*. The bulldog, whose bowl is beaded at its point of greatest circumference, has both a scholarly and rakish air that sartorially suits the college student given to sweaters and gray flannels. Angle the bulldog's shank a few degrees and you have the Scotch Pug, a pipe that subtly sets off the professor's vest and Phi Beta Kappa key.

Their fashion qualities also suggest that pipes may be used to better advantage in decorating—particularly for the bachelor's apartment. Pipes lying about the house afford esthetic pleasure and serve as conversation pieces. And one who aspires to gracious hostdom might provide spare pipes for guests, with an eye toward giving novice smokers instruction on the properties and proprieties of the burning bowl.

What is more delightful than to sit with a rich and delicately veined pipe before a fireplace in which fragrant wood is burning, and spin yarns of high adventure in far-off places? Or, when the company is intimate, to sit and smoke in silence—with only the hiss and pop of the logs to punctuate one's thoughts?

Not enough attention has been given to the pipe smoker's manner, or style, as he holds and uses his pipe. This can be as great an art and as esthetic as the pouring of tea in Japan—and, indeed, may reveal the personality of the whole man. Never fidget with a pipe. Hold it quietly, lovingly, and unostentatiously, as though born with one in hand. Observe any English actor who has true presence, with pipe in mouth or simply resting in hand. What does he do? Virtually nothing. He makes smoking seem as natural as breathing—the pipe seems a mere appendage to his hand. Yet next time you see him, try to estimate how much this seemingly innocent dexterity adds to his charm!

However, one can overdo. The smoker should avoid affectation and mannerisms or he will run the risk of being identified as one of the following kinds of pipe smokers, as tabulated by a 17th-century writer:

The smoker who sends forth smoke from both corners of the mouth in two divergent puffs is crochety and hard to get along with though he may have good mental faculties.

The man who after lighting his pipe holds it not only between teeth and lips but with his hand is fastidious and possessed of much personal pride. Such a smoker will often remove the pipe and examine its bowl to see if it is burning evenly and steadily. Such actions indicate carefulness, sagacity and a character worthy of confidence and esteem.

Men of quick, vivacious temper hardly touch the bit of their pipe to their mouth when, after taking two or three whiffs, they remove it and hold it in their hand in absentminded fashion. They are men who change their opinions and ambitions often and require the spur of novelty to make them exert their best powers.

The smoker who grips his pipe so firmly between his teeth that marks are left on the mouthpiece is mettlesome, of quick, nervous temper and likes to be tenacious of his opinions one way or another.

The pipe held so that it hangs somewhat toward the chin indicates the listless, ambitionless person who might stand up to such responsibilities as come to him but would never seek them or strive for high place.

The man who fills his pipe slowly and methodically and smokes mechanically and regularly is likely to be reserved, prudent and a good dependable friend, while not of a showy exterior.

And now we come to another example of pipe etiquette, or in this case something more—protocol. Old King Cole called for his pipe! Then came his bowl (and even the nursery rhyme does not suggest it contained milk), and last came his fiddlers. How could one do better than imitate a king? It is merry and convivial to light one's pipe and then, when the tobacco is hot and burning, raise a glass and enjoy a drink. Rum and briar pipes are a perfect combination; their bouquet is eminently compatible. For nondrinkers (or at nonalcoholic times) both coffee and tea go nicely with the pipe. To drink milk while smoking a pipe shows a rather feeble appreciation of the esthetics of smoking. Such a combination is more sophomoric than soporific and seems to this writer almost as questionable as the Spanish custom of pouring chocolate over sardines.

The true pipe smoker is not antic, but observes the laws of good manners. He is worthy of his pipe for he knows how, where, and when to smoke it.

The subject of when to smoke has received scant attention—but understandably so, for a man generally smokes a pipe when he feels like doing so. But this early rhyme leaves little doubt that the pipe may be enjoyed from breakfast orange juice to bedtime nightcap:

> *A pipe at nine*
> *Is always fine.*
> *A puff at noon*
> *Is none too soon.*
> *A pipe at three*
> *The thing for me.*
> *A pipe at seven*
> *An aroma to heaven.*
> *A pipe at nine*
> *Is half divine.*
> *A pipe before slumber*
> *Makes just the right number.*

For sheer elegance this description from *A Paper of Tobacco*, published in London in 1839, of a fitting time for a pipe must rate as a top contender: "How soothing is a pipe to the wearied sportsman on his return to the inn from the moors! As he sits quietly smoking, he thinks of the absent friends whom he will gratify with presents of grouse; and, in a perfect state of contentment with himself and all the world, he determines to give all his game away."

Perhaps the one shortcut to mastery of the pipe

is to cultivate a true appreciation of it by reading the rich—and sometimes roisterous—literature of the pipe. Literary aficionados of the pipe have included such able authors as Thackeray, famous for this quotation, "The pipe draws wisdom from the lips of the philosopher and shuts up the mouth of the foolish; it generates a style of conversation contemplative, thoughtful, benevolent and unaffected."

If such words do not entice a man to read further on the pleasures of learning how to smoke a pipe, he is, herewith, advised to forsake or forego the pipe. Let him enlist in the army of cigarette smokers that has been reproved by the Surgeon General. But if he is impelled to go on to pipe mastery, let him remember, above all, that it is good manners, good taste, and good sense that provide the criteria for establishing smokers' rules.

CHAPTER 12

PIPE SMOKING
FOR WOMEN

A PREDICTION: in the world of the future, and perhaps a not too distant future, there will be as many female pipe smokers as there will be male!

Although such a prophecy may offend the ancient fraternity of pipe lovers, it should not evoke surprise. Depending on one's point of view, these past few decades have witnessed repeated efforts by women to "invade man's world," or to assert their right to that much-belabored phrase "sexual equality." That women, in their pursuit of the pleasures that were once entirely male prerogatives, have enjoyed great success is at once evident when one surveys the trophies won by them in recent years. They have established their right to handle golf club and bowling ball, skeet gun and casting rod, sports car and parachute.

In view of the great number of female cigarette smokers in the United States, estimated as being close to 30,000,000, it is astonishing that the day of the "his and hers" pipe set has been so long delayed.

Throughout history women have flirted with the pipe and have played an all-important role in the social evolution of smoking. The earliest visitors to the New World observed women smoking pipes, and there is reason to believe that much earlier the Mayans and Aztecs had their belles of the bowl. In

1561, upon receiving tobacco plants from Jean Nicot, no less a person than Catherine de Medici took
to snuff. The very first botanical book on tobacco
was dedicated to Queen Elizabeth in 1570 by two
London doctors, Pena and Lobel, though there is no
evidence that the lady herself was addicted.

Of course, civilized woman's reaction to the pipe
has not always been favorable. When, in 1588, Sir
Walter Raleigh smoked his pipe in Robert Aston's
park, it is written that "the ladies quit him till he
had done." And yet in the mid-1600's a visiting
Frenchman wrote, of a dinner party in England,
"The dinner being finished, they set on the table
half-a-dozen pipes and a packet of tobacco for
smoking . . . a general custom as well with women
as with men who think that one cannot live without
tobacco because it dissipates the evil humors of the
brain." In 1650 an English poet went on record
with: "Tobacco engages both sexes, all ages."

In France, according to some historians, several
of the Bourbon queens were in the habit of indulg-
ing in a pipe from time to time. Before the Revolution, it is said that on at least one occasion the
Dauphin surprised some of the young princesses
experimenting with the tobacco pipes belonging to
the Swiss Guards. Madame de Pompadour was a
devotee of the pipe, as were the painters Elisabeth
Vigee-Lebrun and, later, Rosa Bonheur. George
Sand, of course, was a notorious smoker, though the
annals of the time leave one uncertain as to whether
she reserved pipe smoking for her appearances in
male dress or, impartially, indulged with equal

pleasure while dressed as a woman who had nothing to do (for not even the Chinese had yet invented the automobile or television), lolled about, exchanging gossip, and inhaling the smoke from a water pipe. And on this side of the world, going back to the days of staunch Quakerdom, we have a record of George Fox's stepdaughter Sarah Fell buying pipes and tobacco for her sister Susannah. It was not uncommon for Quakeresses to smoke. British historian Apperson reports that aboard a ship that sailed in 1765 and carried Quaker passengers, the "Women's Chest" contained "Balm, sage, summer Savoury, horehound, Tobaccao and Oranges, two bottles of brandy, two bottles of Jamaica spirrit, A cannister of green tea, a jar of almond paste, ginger bread and a box of pipes."

In some parts of this country the corncob attained a well-documented popularity with women. At the time of Andrew Jackson's presidency, many stories were circulated about Mrs. Jackson's reluctance to leave her corncob behind when she moved to the White House.

Pipes were all but banished from milady's boudoir when grumpy Queen Victoria ascended the throne. Nevertheless, some diehards remained. In the year 1845, 96-year-old Molly Pheasy, a crone as addicted to the pipe as to the teapot, set fire to her clothes while lighting up a pipe. Soon after, another grand dame of the pipe passed on: Jane Garbutt who at the age of 110 had, according to her own diary, "dwindled into a small compass, but she was free from pain, retaining all her faculties to the last and enjoying her pipe."

In 1877 Andrew Steinmetz, in his *Smoker's Guide*, gleefully recounts this anecdote:

It appears that the Countess of A————, with a laudable desire to promote tidiness in the different cottages on her estate in Scotland, used to visit them periodically and exhort the inmates to cleanliness. One cottage was always found especially untidy, and the Countess at length took up a broom and having by its use made an improvement, said to the housewife who was meanwhile enjoying her pipe—"Now my good woman, is this not much better?" "Oh, ay, my leddy," said the matron, presenting her pipe to the Countess, "an wull ye tak' a blast noo?"

By the latter part of the 1800's, though the cigarette had captured the fancy of the continent, it appears that there were still women, chiefly among the lower classes, loyal to the pipe, as evidenced by this old Seven Dials ballad:

When I first saw Miss Bailey,
'Twas on Saturday,
At the Corner Pin she was drinking gin,
And smoking a yard of clay.

In 1913, in Scotland, a woman who was brought to police court and charged with drunkenness put the blame for her unsteady gait upon her pipe, contending that though she had smoked her pipe for nearly 20 years, "it always makes me giddy." At about this time the magazine *Punch*, a caustic and conservative censor of British fashion, registered alarm at the increasing popularity of smoking among women of the middle and upper classes. In a picture drawn by Leach, and captiously titled "A Quiet Smoke," five women were shown in a tobacconist's shop, two smoking cigars and two smoking pipes, while "one of the inferior animals" sold tobacco behind the counter.

Queen Victoria, that notorious tobaccophobe, once received a gift of pipes and tobacco from the King of Dahomey, head of a West African state to whom the Queen had sent a damask tent, two silver trays, and a silver pipe. Accepting these items from Sir Richard Burton, the Queen's courier, the Dahomey King commented that the tent was too small, the silver pipe was not as satisfactory as his old wooden-stemmed redclay, and the trays were not nearly big enough to use as shields. Perhaps to underscore the disappointment that attends the receipt of an unsuitable gift, the King sent Queen Victoria the pipes and tobacco, an umbrella, and an array of fabrics, along with the suggestion that the Queen's next gift to him include a carriage and horses and a white woman.

The fanatical feminists of the early part of the 20th century proved to be uncompromising foes of the pipe. Chief among them was Carrie Nation, arrested in 1907 in Washington for disorderly conduct while inveighing against the evils of tobacco, and quoted two years later as insisting that fog is God's vengeance upon tobacco smokers.

Not until 1927 did a cigarette manufacturer dare to place an advertisement showing a woman actually smoking. At that, the caption was a masterpiece of caution, murmuring, "Women—when they smoke at all—quickly develop discerning taste." That era found cigarette manufacturers coaxing women to smoke cigarettes made with colored papers, fragile scents, and exotic tips of gold leaf, silk, linen, satinwood, and pastel straw. The persuasion was effective enough, though women did not respond (do they ever?) as the manufacturers expected. They cast their vote for he-man brands of cigarettes, eschewing the effete products designed for their consumption and delighting in blends nearly as dizzying as those violent concoctions that once burned in the pipes of our sea-voyaging Quaker ancestresses.

This turn of events brings us again to the question: Why, then, has the pipe not caught on with distaff smokers? The most obvious and cogent reason is that the pipe itself was, until quite recently, in general decline throughout the world. Secondly, the pipe industry itself must be taken to task for not following the suit of other industries—notably the producers of automobiles and sporting goods—and making the most of modern manufacturing, advertising, and merchandising methods, including such advanced techniques as ikonogenics and motivational research, to woo American womankind.

The recent market debut of bejewelled briar pipes similar to those once popular at court suggests that pipe makers have, at least, emerged from their Rip van Winkle phase. Publicizing, promotion, and advertising of pipes adorned with rhinestones, semi-precious stones, pastel cameos, etc., represents a significant stride forward. But it may be that the most help will come from the most unlikely ally—the cigarette.

Although not as awesome as the evidence that links cigarette smoking to cancer in American males, the facts pertaining to cigarette smoking's causal relationship to diseases in American females is, nonetheless, frightening, and few psychiatrists would deny that women may yet react accordingly; unfathomable as women may appear to be at times, they are also inclined to be more sensible and practical about their health than men.

If the risks attributed to smoking cigarettes do not win female converts for the pipe, it may be that women will be enticed by the pipe's fashion qualities, their greater opportunities for decoration and ornamentation. They may assume any shape and size. They may be jewelled, covered with lizard skin, coated with chinchilla, or strewn with ceramic rose buds. It is conceivable that teen-age girls who wish to take up smoking without becoming habituated to inhaling cigarettes might become excited over pipes decorated with carvings or pictures of current idols, such as the Beatles. Pipes might lend themselves to the mirroring of many fads; properly decorated with tribal insignia, as once were the pipes of German students, they could assume the same significance as an identifying badge on the lapel.

On the subject of pipe tobacco itself, it would seem, on the basis of women's expressed preferences in cigarettes, that the pipe tobaccos favored by men would enjoy the same popularity among women. In all likelihood, experienced women smokers would find feminized pipe tobaccos—particularly if they were blended to resemble the bouquet of certain after-dinner liqueurs, not to mention colognes and perfumes—odious, if not downright repugnant.

Approached on the grounds of health, fashion, and fad, with encouragement from modern advertising and merchandising techniques, it seems that it can be only a matter of time before women perceive that there is no reason why the pipe should remain so predominantly a masculine prerogative, and discover for themselves the pleasure that comes from knowing how to smoke a pipe.

A female pipe smoker would be well advised, however, not to be completely a victim of fad in her choice of pipes. Some of those pipes offered for sale to women are short of stem and thimble-sized of bowl—they confuse "cuteness" with beauty and utility. Such pipes will burn hot, to biting the tongue and choking the nostrils with smoke. A woman truly interested in converting to a pipe will make a better choice than one of those—to begin with, surely, a briar of pleasing shape and size.

Male pipe smokers, wishing to encourage their wives to join them in their enjoyment, can have

recourse to this persuasive advice to women offered by an early marriage counselor: "Ye Wives
(of England), why, as you cannot help ruffling
your husbands—as you are made to please and not
tease them—deny them not the pipe, which you can
make the bond of union and loving kindness between you. . . . As your husband smokes his pipe,
so smoke *you*, imparting preservation to your
charms—to your fascination endless omnipotence."
Clearly, the suggestion is that a woman who loves
her pipe-smoking husband will return his love by
joining him in a smoke. The day of "his and her"
pipe sets may be closer than we think.

GLOSSARY

Here are some of the names, words, and phrases that the author believes are likely to arouse the pipe smoker's curiosity as he browses among tobacco shops and through the literature of the pipe:

Absorbents: This word is occasionally applied to the cloth or synthetic filters found in some makes of pipe.

Adrianople: A popular blending agent used in pipe tobacco, this neutral-flavored tobacco is grown on the plains of Turkey.

Aging: The process of mellowing tobacco that has been cured by storing it in casks known as hogsheads.

Air-curing: Generally, this is the process of curing tobacco in barns by controlled ventilation rather than by use of artificial heat. Most of the tobaccos from Virginia, Kentucky, and Maryland are air-cured.

Air-drying: The process of drying tobacco by the use of natural air.

Alderman: This is an Old English word for the long, once-popular Yard of Clay pipe. The pipe was so long that the owner could rest the bowl on the arm of his chair.

Algonquin pipe: Made of wood, bone or stone, the pipe was essentially a tube. Many have been dug up in the celebrated burial mounds of Ohio and Virginia.

Anatolian: A Turkish tobacco used in pipe blends. Other names for it are Broussa, Dusdje, Hendek, Gonen, and Ismid.

Apooke: An Indian name for Virginia tobacco, recorded by Strachey who wrote, in 1610, "Here is a great store of tobacco which the savages call apooke." He said the savages smoke "the same in pipes of earth, which very ingeniously they make."

Auction: The means by, or place at, which tobacco is sold to the highest bidder.

Aya-Solouk: The Smyrna region famed for its highly aromatic Turkish tobaccos.

Baai: The coarse Java leaf tobacco smoked by Netherlanders in their big clay pipes.

Baffra: A Turkish blending agent for pipe tobaccos grown near Baffra. It compares somewhat with Samsoun, though the leaf does not have a stem.

Bahia: A sweet, mild tobacco found in the Brazilian province of Bahia, famous for its many Brazilian tobaccos.

Bar: Tobacco—especially Cavendish—pressed into the shape of a bar and encased by a wrapper leaf.

Basibali: One of the principal kinds of Turkish tobacco.

Basma: A pressed tobacco as important as Basibali.

Bent: A pipe with a round bowl into which the

shank is fitted at a 45° angle and joined to a stem that is quite noticeably curved.

Bird's eye: A hard, sweet, and very fine tobacco popular in Great Britain. Also a pattern of grain found on some briar pipes.

Bit: The part of the pipe stem that fits in the mouth. It is called the mouthpiece in England.

Body: The weight and density of tobacco leaf.

Boer: A pipe with a shank so thick that it seems to be a projection of the bowl. Curving from the upper part of the bowl, the shank usually accommodates a straight stem.

Boiler: A derisive term for a pipe.

Bowl: The part of the pipe that contains the tobacco. It may or may not have an independent stem.

Brazilian: A perique that is cut very fine.

Briar: That part of the white heather tree called burl and used for the manufacture of briar pipes. The Mediterranean yields highly prized briar.

Briar pipe: A pipe made from briar.

Bulldog: A square-shanked pipe. Squat and solid-looking, the pipe employs a saddle-type bit and a square stem the length of the bowl and shank. The bowl is usually beaded at its widest point.

Bull Moose: A rather short pipe. The shank is very heavy and curves slightly, as does the stem, with the result that the bit is even with the top of the bowl.

Burley: Usually refers to white Burley, though Red, Twist Bud, and other varieties were once popular. Burley is an air-cured tobacco suited to pipe blends. Kentucky, Ohio, and Tennessee are leading Burley producers.

Cachimba: A type of Cuban pipe.

Calabash: A bowl of meerschaum—or occasionally clay—set into the bulbous part of a specially prepared gourd, which has been fitted with a mouthpiece.

Calumet: The Indian peace pipe.

Cavendish: Tobacco that has been impregnated with a sweetening agent, for instance, maple syrup. Cavendish is most often Virginia leaf that is molded into bars or cakes, then cut.

Celtic Pipe: Tiny clay pipes dug up in various parts of Ireland. The pipes belong to the Elizabethan era.

Churchwarden: An English clay pipe with a stem of unusual length, often a foot or more. They were the graceful successors to the long 17th-century pipes.

Clay: A clay pipe. Clays have been manufactured since the North American Indians discovered that clay—a common, plastic material obtained from the soil—lends itself readily to pipe making.

Club: A short-stemmed pipe with a round bowl and a long, often oval, shank.

Coal: A live ember of coal or wood used to light a pipe. It was the common device for lighting pipes in the 16th and 17th centuries.

Cohoba: A powdery form of tobacco once smoked by South American Indians in a tubed bowl that could be used by two persons simultaneously. In the West Indies Cohoba was for many years the popular name for tobacco.

Common tobacco: This term usually refers to *nicotiana rustica*, especially in England, where the plant is common in private gardens.

Condenser: Often called a fitment or extension, it is the part of the pipe that projects into the tenon and shank. Tars, nicotine, moisture, and impurities are condensed in this way.

Cure: The means by which the natural sap in tobacco is removed. Flues, fires, and the heat from the sun may be used, depending on the type of tobacco.

Curve: A pipe with a completely curved stem. So daringly does the stem curve that the bit is usually perpendicular to the bowl.

Cuts: A British word for pipe tobaccos, as well as other smoking tobaccos.

Cutty: In Scottish, the word means *short* and, in pipe circles, refers to a kind of pipe that is less than three inches long.

Dark shag: A tobacco, processed in bars, that is heated before being cut. One kind of dark shag is Cavendish.

Deer's-tongue: A flavoring agent for pipe tobaccos. It is also used as a substitute for vanilla. The herb grows best in the southeast part of the U.S.

Divine herb: A name given tobacco in Europe when it was thought to have miraculous medicinal properties.

Djebel: A Turkish tobacco used in blends.

Dottle: The unburned tobacco that cakes in a bowl.

Drinking tobacco: An archaic term for smoking and, especially, inhaling.

Dry Smoke: Slang for an unlighted smoke. Can refer to cigarette and cigar as well as a pipe.

Dudeen: Much like the Scottish cutty, this Irish pipe is also extremely short, generally less than three inches in length.

Dutch wine pipe: A porcelain pipe with two bowls. Wine is poured into the lower bowl and flavors the smoke. A long pipe that descends sharply from mouth to chest or even to waist level, the Dutch wine pipe is usually exquisitely painted.

Ecume de Mer: French word for meerschaum. Literal translation is "sea foam."

Elfin Pipe: Small clay pipes dug up in Scotland and, like the Celtic pipes of Ireland, often romantically and superstitiously linked to fairies.

Ferrule: The metal ring or band around the pipe's shank.

Fillin's: Folksy slang for pipe tobacco.

Filter: An aluminum device, cloth pad, cotton wool tube, or similar device inserted in the pipe to trap nicotine, tars, etc. Charcoal, asbestos, meerschaum—a wide variety of materials have been employed. System and fitment are common synonyms for filter.

Fine cut: Tobacco that has been finely shredded. Usually smokes quickly—and hot.

Fire curing: One of the oldest methods of curing tobacco, it is a means of using smoke to dry tobacco.

Flake: Tobacco cut into fine, though irregular, pieces that smoke fast.

Flame grain: A distinctive pattern on briarwood.

Flash: The brightness or brilliant coloring of certain flue-cured tobaccos.

Flavor: The taste and/or aroma of a tobacco, usually imparted by artificial agents used to improve the natural flavor of tobacco leaf.

Flue curing: The use of pipes, called flues, to radiate heat and dry tobacco.

Foom: Mouthpiece for an Egyptian pipe, made of pieces of amber joined by gold, jewels, etc.

Gouda: A Dutch city known for the manufacture of world-famous Dutch pipes and the site of the country's pottery industry. The wrath of James I forced many skilled English pipe makers to settle in Gouda.

Gourd: The vegetable used in the manufacture of calabash pipes.

Gozeh: The poor man's narghile, this Persian water pipe has a very short stem and lacks a stand.

Grand Prieur, l'herbe de: A French word for tobacco, used some centuries ago.

Granulated: Very coarsely cut smoking tobacco used in pipe blends.

Harvesting: The reaping of tobacco, which can be accomplished in either of two ways: priming, or picking leaves from the plant as each leaf becomes ripe; and stalk-cutting, or cutting down the whole plant.

Heel: The bottom, or base, of the inside of a pipe bowl. *Heel* is often confused with *dottle,* which means the wet, unburned tobacco in a pipe bowl.

Henbane: The English coined this word for the tobacco used by Indians. The Indians smoked *nicotiana rusticana* and *nicotiana tabacum.*

Hhagar: An Egyptian pipe bowl of baked earth. The bowl is usually red or brown.

Hogshead: A cask of tobacco weighing approximately 1,000 pounds. Tobacco is stored—and sometimes sold—in hogsheads.

Hookah: A water-cooled pipe, also called Hubble-Bubble and Narghile. In Arabic, *Hookah* means round box or casket. Hookah may also refer to the tobacco, a mixture of Khambira and other Turkish tobaccos, smoked in the long-stemmed pipe.

Hubble-Bubble: An onomatopoetic word for Hookah.

Indian Drug: A 17th-century term referring to tobacco as a herb with medicinal properties.

Kabakolak: A Turkish tobacco sometimes used in pipe tobacco blends.

Kalian: Another word for the Persian water pipe or Hookah.

Kaloup: Those less select leaves of Turkish tobacco that do not come from the top part of the tobacco plant.

Khambira: A blend of Turkish tobacco flavored with fruit that has been allowed to ferment in an earthen vessel buried underground.

Killikinnick: Once a trade name, it generally refers now to any kind of granulated tobacco.

Kiniikinnick: Indian word for a mixed tobacco.

Latakia: An open-fire-cured tobacco from Syria that is one of the most popular flavoring agents used in pipe blends. It is dark in color—often nearly black—and distinctive in taste.

Leaf: Tobacco as it appears before entering advanced manufacturing processes. Also, upper leaves of the plant. Sometimes used to mean the heavier parts of certain Burley tobaccos.

Macedonian: Turkish tobaccos often used to flavor pipe blends.

Mannzanita: Burl from a California plant sometimes used in place of briar for pipe making.

Meerschaum: A mineral substance that is carved into pipes. The best grades are found in Asia Minor.

Meerschaum pipes: Pipes made from meerschaum. They are prized for their light weight and coloring qualities.

Missouri Meerschaum: Slang for a pipe made from a corncob.

Moose: See Bull Moose.

Mound pipes: Pipes buried in mounds of earth by the Indians of the Mississippi Valley. Carved to resemble people and animals, the pipes were often as hard and brittle as porcelain.

Mouthpiece: Another word for bit, often used by the British.

Narghile (or Nargileh): A word now used to refer to almost any of the water pipes popular in Persia, East Africa, or the East Indies. The word means coconut, which is the material of the vessel used to contain the water through which the smoke is filtered.

Navy Plug: A grade of slightly sweetened Burley once very popular with sailors aboard ship.

Nicotiana: The name for tobacco that honors Jean Nicot, widely credited with having introduced tobacco to Europe.

Nicotiana Persica: A tobacco native to Persia that bears white flowers.

Nicotiana Rustica: The tobacco raised in Virginia by the Indians. John Rolfe, however, encouraged the colonists to raise *Nicotiana tabacum*, which has a much superior taste. Now the term commonly refers to Syrian tobacco as distinguished from tobacco raised in America.

Nicotiana tabacum: Virginia tobacco, an impressive plant with a height of six or seven feet and leaves two feet long.

Nose Warmer: Slang for a very short pipe.

Oleoresin: The combination of oil and resin that greatly influences the combustibility and taste of a tobacco.

Oom-Paul: A style of pipe with a large bowl. So sharply curved are the stem and shank of the pipe that the bit stands three times the height of the bowl when the pipe is upright.

Peace pipe: Pipes used ceremonially, especially in negotiating peace treaties, and principally by Indians of the Plains region. Also called calumet.

Perfumes: Flavoring agents used in some blended pipe tobaccos, these include such oils and perfumes as anise, cinnamon, cloves, menthol, nutmeg, and peppermint. Less frequently used perfumes are bois de rose, cascarilla, cassia, gentian root, sandalwood, valerian, and rosemary.

Perique: A Louisiana tobacco with the strongest flavor of any currently grown. It is cured in its own juices and widely used in flavoring aromatic pipe tobaccos.

Pipe mark: The insignia, initials, or name of a pipe manufacturer of clay pipes in England during the 17th and 18th centuries.

Pipe-walk: Referred to the "beat" or route of London vendors of pipes that enabled them to call on each of their customers.

Plug: Tobacco twisted or pressed into cakes, then shredded for use as pipe tobacco.

Prince of Wales: A pipe with a short, rather fat bowl and a gently curved stem and shank that give the pipe a graceful look.

Pudding: An early term for tobacco that was processed into a roll. The pudding, sometimes called a "cane," was often made by the village apothecary.

Quality: Tobacco is graded by type of leaf and by quality, which is determined by the tobacco's uniformity, texture, age, oil, body, coloring, etc. The five grades are: choice, fine, good, fair, and low.

Raleigh, Sir Walter: Believed to be the first to smoke a pipe in England, he popularized smoking at the court of Queen Elizabeth.

Raw: Tobacco after it has been harvested and before it has been cured.

Resin: A component of oleoresin added to pipe tobaccos to improve flavor and influence combustibility.

Samsoun: One of the most popular of Turkish tobaccos used in pipe blends. Reddish-brown or yellow in color, the leaf produces a distinctive aroma.

Sayri: A word—nearly 500 years old—for the tobacco smoked by certain of the Peruvian Indians.

Scotch Pug: A square-shanked, square-bowled pipe with a marked resemblance to the Bulldog. Unlike the Bulldog, its shank angles up from the bottom of the bowl.

Seesheh: A style of Persian water pipe employing a glass bowl to contain the water through which the smoke is filtered. *Seesheh,* an Arabic word, means *glass.*

Shadegrown: A word, of little consequence to the pipe smoker, for shade-grown tobacco—that raised under canopies that eliminate direct sunlight. It is used almost exclusively in the manufacture of leaf for cigar making.

Shag: A finely shredded though coarse tobacco found in many commercial pipe blends.

Shank: The element of the pipe that connects bowl and stem. When bowl and shank are one and the same piece, the term used is *pipehead.*

Sickle: A style of pipe resembling the Woodstock but having a more sharply curved stem. The bit rises above the top of the pipe bowl, though much less than that of the Oom-Paul.

Smokestack: Derogatory slang for a pipe.

Smyrna: A popular Turkish tobacco used for flavoring pipe tobacco blends. It tends to burn poorly.

Sokia: A Turkish tobacco grown in the Smyrna area and famed as one of the most aromatic of the Turkish tobaccos.

Stem: That part of the pipe that connects shank with bit. It is sometimes mistakenly called the mouthpiece.

Stud: A pot bowl pipe, one with a round, flat-bottomed bowl and straight stem.

Stummel: The shank and bowl of a briar or of a wooden pipe, called Ebauchon in France.

Sweet-S(c)ented: Considered one of the finest tobaccos of Colonial Virginia, the tobacco was a strain of *Nicotiana tabacum.*

Tobagies: Shops in old England where smokers gathered to discuss pipes and tobacco and to exchange news of the day.

Tenon: That part of the pipe stem that projects to fit into the shank, forming an airtight joint.

Tobacco: Plants belonging to the family *Solanaceae.* Members include the tomato and potato plants. The genus *Nicotiana* is native to this country. There are probably some 40 kinds of tobacco known to botanists and at least 26 standardized types of leaf recognized and defined by the Department of Agriculture.

Tobago: An island that Columbus named in 1498 in honor, according to one story, of the shape of a Carib pipe he observed there.

Toombak: A Persian tobacco smoked in a damp state in the narghile or seesheh. Live coals are placed on top of the Toombak to light it.

Trebizond: An aromatic tobacco grown in Turkey and used almost exclusively for the blending of pipe tobaccos.

Tube: One of the earliest forms of pipes. It consisted of a cylinder, sometimes "filtered" with a pipe that stopped tobacco dust from passing into the smoker's mouth.

Tumblin's: Slang for tobacco for a pipe, it sometimes applies to cigarette tobacco.

Turkish: The air-cured tobaccos raised in Turkey and imported by the U.S., as well as other countries, for use in the blending of pipe and other tobaccos. Turkish tobacco raised in the uplands is called *yaka*, and that in the lowlands, *ova*.

Tyrolean pipe: A large wooden pipe popular in Alpine countries. Its bit—usually made of bone—and shank are quite long, putting the bowl at chest height. The bowl is often finely carved and nearly always topped with a ventilated lid.

Water pipe, Oriental: Many forms exist, of which the earliest, dating back to the late 15th century, were probably used to smoke hemp rather than tobacco.

Wellington: A distinctive style of pipe with a rounded bowl and diamond-shaped stem fastened to the shank with a large ferrule.

Woodstock: A funnel-shaped bowl gives this pipe the appearance of the Sickle, though the curve of its stem and shank are less pronounced.

Yard of Clay: A very long clay pipe popular in 19th-century England because its length permitted the smoker to rest the bowl on the arm of his chair. The Dutch also favored these pipes, which were sometimes known as Aldermen.